The
Contemplative
Response

The Bible Reading Fellowship
15 The Chambers, Vineyard
Abingdon OX14 3FE
brf.org.uk

The Bible Reading Fellowship (BRF) is a Registered Charity (233280)

ISBN 978 0 85746 656 3
First published 2019
10 9 8 7 6 5 4 3 2 1 0
All rights reserved

Acknowledgements
Unless otherwise acknowledged, scripture quotations are taken from The New Revised
Standard Version of the Bible, Anglicised edition, copyright © 1989, 1995 by the Division of
Christian Education of the National Council of the Churches of Christ in the United States of
America. Used by permission. All rights reserved.

Scripture quotations marked RSV are taken from The Revised Standard Version of the Bible,
copyright © 1946, 1952, 1971 by the Division of Christian Education of the National Council of
the Churches of Christ in the United States of America. Used by permission. All rights reserved.

Extracts from the Authorised Version of the Bible (The King James Bible), the rights in which
are vested in the Crown, are reproduced by permission of the Crown's Patentee, Cambridge
University Press.

'Brilliant Disguise', 'Spare Parts' and 'When You're Alone' by Bruce Springsteen. Copyright
© 1987 Bruce Springsteen (Global Music Rights). Reprinted by permission. International
copyright secured. All rights reserved.

'Hungry Heart' by Bruce Springsteen. Copyright © 1980 Bruce Springsteen (Global Music
Rights). Reprinted by permission. International copyright secured. All rights reserved.

'Human Touch' by Bruce Springsteen. Copyright © 1992 Bruce Springsteen (Global Music
Rights). Reprinted by permission. International copyright secured. All rights reserved.

Canon Rich Simpson, 'Meet Me Out in the Street'. Used by permission.

Every effort has been made to trace and contact copyright owners for material used in
this resource. We apologise for any inadvertent omissions or errors, and would ask those
concerned to contact us so that full acknowledgement can be made in the future.

A catalogue record for this book is available from the British Library

Printed and bound in Great Britain by Clays Ltd, Elcograf S.p.A.

The
Contemplative
Response

Leadership and ministry
in a distracted culture

Ian Cowley

Acknowledgements

Thank you to all those who have walked alongside me over these past years and helped to make this book possible. Thank you, Alison, for standing with me through it all. To all my family and friends, to everyone who has worked on this book, thank you for your encouragement, help and support. This book would not have been written without you.

Mike Parsons at BRF opened the door for me to write a follow-up to *The Contemplative Minister*, and the whole BRF team have been wonderfully helpful and supportive. Diane Faux did a huge amount of the hard work in turning my scribbling into documents. I learnt so much from The Contemplative Minister team in the Diocese of Salisbury: Sue Langdon, Peter Greenwood and Darrell Weyman. Many friends helped with comments and advice along the way, especially Steve Pearson, Andrew Judge, Philip Dale, Pat Dale, Bridget Holding and Grace Kennedy.

I am very grateful to Madeleine Bransby and the staff at Oakham School library for generously offering me access to the Merton Collection and a place to think and write.

Thank you, God, for from your hand you have given us freely and abundantly of your steadfast mercy, goodness and love.

Contents

Foreword

At one point in this book, Ian Cowley speaks of the effort we put into the 'avoidance of depth' in our action and awareness. The most serious challenge his discussion puts before us is the question of where we act from in our engagement with the world around us, human and non-human. If we act from the levels of our being that are closest to the surface, most bound up with our self-image and our appearance in the eyes of others, we condemn ourselves to continuing unreality, with all the damage it brings to ourselves and to other beings. If we act from somewhere closer to the centre, we are likely to open the way to something more creative and healing. Yet we are so in love with those surface pictures and habits that we can put immense energy into – in effect – maintaining a lie.

Ian meets the reader where that reader is (this reader, certainly) and sets out candidly his own moments of hard self-discovery, as well as his counsel for how we might allow God simply to be God in us and for us. To discover something of the contemplative path is to discover something about God: we recognise the strange idol we have set up, the product of the panic, vanity and neediness that come so readily to us; and we learn how to open ourselves to the actuality of a God who is immeasurably more than what our emotional dramas can generate. The movement closer to the true God is also a movement closer to a 'true self' – not – emphatically not – some little core of pure individuality buried inside, but a being free and ready to be nourished by truth, not by image and fantasy.

If we are able to take a step in this direction, we become not more isolated from the world of tough decisions and moral dilemmas, but less eager to run away or hide or pretend. 'The truth will set you free,' says Jesus; he, who always acts out of the depth of his relation to the God of Israel whom he calls 'Father', lives, dies and rises so that we may be drawn deeper into his own true and just connection with what is eternally real. Our prayer and our actions alike must reflect our trust in the reality and power of this gift.

And so if we are trying to be truthful ministers of the gospel, this is the truthfulness we must seek to model and to share. Ian diagnoses with sharp insight the compulsions that will take us away from this and offers simple and lucid guidance for growing in trust. This is a life-giving reflection; may the readers who need it find it.

Rowan Williams
Master of Magdalene College, Cambridge,
and former Archbishop of Canterbury

Introduction

Blessed are the
pure in heart

It is always a slightly awkward and uncomfortable conversation:
'Didn't you know? He has had to withdraw from public ministry for a
while.' 'Oh! I am sorry. When did this happen?' It is difficult to know
what questions to ask or what to say next.

Recently, a number of my colleagues in ministry and leadership
have had to resign because of disciplinary or personal issues. My
response to this is always one of sadness, prayer and concern for
the churches involved, for the families and for the person who has
had to step down from a leadership role under difficult and troubling
circumstances.

This has led me to reflect on my own inner life, and the ways in which
I tend to respond to the demands and pressures of public ministry.
In recent years I have become increasingly aware of my own desires
for power and control, for safety and security and for esteem and
significance, and of the ways in which these desires are able to rule
my heart. Control, security and esteem are important for all of us if
we are to survive and flourish. But to become the person that God
has made me and called me to be, I need to learn to let go of these
desires. I can, if I am willing, learn instead to trust and to allow God
to rule my heart and to be my peace and the provider of my needs.
The state of my heart before God is the key to my ability to deal well
with the temptations and pressures of life in leadership.

When I am busy and caught up in my work, these desires are largely
taken care of. Leadership provides plenty of opportunities for me to

be in control, to be secure in my areas of competence and to receive a sense of significance. But when I stop and take time out, I learn some interesting lessons about myself. When I cease from busyness and activity, I discover more fully my own inner restlessness, the internal clamour to keep seeking control, significance and security. So, even though I am away from work, I find that I am still being drawn to acquire more stuff, to achieve more goals and to indulge my appetites. And this is where the problems can arise for many of us.

These are the perennial areas of struggle for Christian leaders. So often it comes back to money and possessions, to sex and drink, and to the workaholic obsession with doing things. I know that I am not immune from the possibility of falling into difficulty in any of these areas. 'There but for the grace of God go I.'

But perhaps the fact that I am aware of my own human weakness is, in fact, a strength. The danger comes when we do not recognise that we are all vulnerable. The real killer so often is denial. Once we tell ourselves, 'It won't happen to me,' or, 'It's not really a problem,' we are in trouble. I have found that it is vital to have a few close friends, as well as a spiritual director or soul friend, to whom I can regularly be accountable. 'Who am I talking to about this?' is an important question for all of us in Christian leadership. This is not just about my prayer life, but about everything that is going on in my life and heart.

An inner truthfulness is also required if we are to grow into holiness. The pruning shears of testing and suffering will be at work in each of us, as Jesus has made clear in the gospels (see John 15:2). When this is happening to us, we will be greatly helped if we have established a daily practice of prayer that is able to address the needs of our hearts for a depth of relationship with the all-loving heart of God. We can also learn to pay proper attention to the God-given rhythms of work and rest, of family and friends, of solitude and society. Then we will find deep within ourselves a growing attentiveness to grace, to the unfailing goodness and mercy of God at work in his people and his creation.

I have recently been reading the DCI Banks series of detective novels by Peter Robinson, set in the Yorkshire Dales. Alan Banks is a good cop, with a deep-seated sense of honour, integrity and commitment to the work to which he is called. He is driven by a strong desire to bring about justice for the victims of some terrible crimes that he has to investigate. He works long hours, and he often seems obsessed.

In the early novels, Alan has a good marriage to Sandra, and two children growing up at home. Slowly his family drifts apart. Suddenly Sandra leaves him, and his marriage is over. But we, the readers, know that this has all been building up for years. We have seen Banks under pressure, away from home, when he 'loses it' and resorts to getting drunk and losing his temper, and becomes open to sexual temptation. His story is the story of many Christian leaders. The truth is that this can happen to any of us, especially if we are living in denial about our own impulses and behaviour patterns.

I have found that facing up to the realities of what is often called 'the false self' and its desires for control, security and esteem has been highly significant for me. I now understand much better where some of my problematic habits and patterns of behaviour are coming from. The false self is the part of who I am that is all about 'me'. This is part of my sinful human nature, the side of my character that is first of all concerned about my interests, my safety and my position in the world. I am slowly learning to look at my 'false self' with compassion, knowing that it no longer needs to be constantly running the show.

The desire of my heart is that I might find my true self and learn to live in the present moment. This is not primarily about seeking control, security and significance. Rather, this means growing into a way of life where being comes before doing. This way of living can gradually lead to contentment with what I have, to compassion for myself and to control over my appetites. I lose the restless need for self-gratification and indulgence, the need to acquire more stuff and to prove myself to those who are 'out there'. The true self finds peace in resting in the love of God, in the peace that Jesus promises. Jesus says to each of us in ministry, 'As the Father has loved me, so I have loved you; abide [rest, dwell] in my love' (John 15:9).

As our culture moves deeper into the 21st century, we find ourselves facing unique challenges. Everywhere around us the world is moving faster. The pressure of constantly responding to an endless flow of information is hard for many of us to handle. We are a distracted and troubled generation, despite all the advances of technology. Jesus calls his followers, especially his ministers, to live as those who are pure in heart, whose hearts are held firm and secure in his peace. 'Peace I leave with you; my peace I give to you. I do not give to you as the world gives. Do not let your hearts be troubled, and do not let them be afraid' (John 14:27).

This is the way of the heart, the contemplative response. In my book *The Contemplative Minister*, I wrote:

> So what is a contemplative? A contemplative person is someone who has learnt to let go, in particular of the desire to be in control and the fear of failing, and who has learnt to listen, to be attentive and to yield to the will of God whatever that may be. Contemplation is an intimacy with God, a wordless resting in God beyond all our thoughts and words and strivings. To be a contemplative people and a contemplative church we must pause from our activity and busyness, to reground our hearts in God, without whom we are nothing.[1]

In this book I have tried to explore a contemplative response to life in the world of the 21st century. What does it mean to be a Christian minister or leader in a world of ceaseless busyness, endless demands and seductive consumerism? What should be the response of any Christian, any follower of Jesus, who seeks to be faithful to Jesus Christ while at the same time being continually faced with the temptations to achieve and do more, to acquire and buy stuff, and to indulge our every appetite? This book will try to point to a way of living in our complex and distracted culture while remaining faithful to Christ, and abiding in his love and care and mercy.

In this book we will look at the demands placed upon our hearts and allegiances in contemporary culture. We will see how easily we can be pulled from safety and into danger by the currents of the ocean in which we swim. We may find ourselves in deep water, desperate to know the real God who alone can save us. To become our true or real selves, we need to find the real God. But there are many false gods and subtle forms of idolatry surrounding us.

To find the real God, the one whose name is Love, we need to recognise the inner compulsions of the false self. The false self places 'me', instead of God, at the centre of everything. I have found that this manifests itself in my desires to acquire, to achieve and to indulge. The remedies for these compulsions are not easy, but they are biblical, and I believe that they are essential for any Christian who is serious about faithfulness to the teaching of Jesus in our culture and society. These remedies are contentment, detachment and self-control.

Finally, we will look at the nature of the contemplative heart. We will see a heart that is attuned and attentive to the presence of God through daily contemplative practice. This is a heart that wrestles with denial and illusion, and reaches out for truthfulness and self-knowledge. We learn to live in the present moment, not being pulled constantly to what has happened in the past or to what we are going to do about the future. We see that contemplation and action are inescapably bound together. 'The closer you get to God, the more you have God's compassionate heart,' says Sister Diana OPB.

The apostle Paul wrote to the Ephesians, 'I pray that, according to the riches of his glory, he may grant that you may be strengthened in your inner being with power through his Spirit, and that Christ may dwell in your hearts through faith, as you are rooted and grounded in love' (Ephesians 3:16–17). My hope and prayer is that this book may help some of us to respond to the demands and the pressures that surround us with pure hearts, hearts that are held firm in the love of God that is Christ Jesus. This is *The Contemplative Response*.

Part One

Choose this day whom you will serve

1

The restless heart

It had been one of those weeks. The diary was already full before the problem with one of our senior leaders. I had to be in London all day on Tuesday, and on Thursday I had promised to go with my wife to visit her father, following her mother's recent death from cancer. There was a series of meetings, all of which I needed to attend. I had a big wedding on Saturday and two major talks to prepare, and I had a nagging health problem that just wouldn't go away.

I arrived home just after six in the evening. I felt tired and stressed, and I knew I still had a couple of hours' work waiting for me in the study. My wife had been out all day teaching. The next thing I knew, a few sharp words had been spoken, and I lost it. I grabbed my mobile phone and threw it across the kitchen as hard as I could. It bounced off the kitchen wall and with a loud crack smashed into three or four pieces on the floor. One classic Nokia phone had reached the end of its life. My wife and I stood looking at one another for a few moments, and then I strode out of the house and climbed into the car and drove away.

I didn't have any idea where I was going. I just had to get out of there, get away from all the pressure, away from all the places where I was required to be strong, to be friendly, to be wise, to be kind and to be in control. I drove out into open green countryside nearby and found a place to stop. I walked for about half an hour, then sat quietly in the car.

Finally feeling more settled, I went home. I said to my wife, 'I'm really sorry. It all just gets too much sometimes.' She looked at me for a while and a sad smile flickered in her eyes. We spent a short time talking, dealing with what had happened. Then we settled down to supper and a quiet evening together. The work could wait for another day.

But I knew that what had happened was not good. I could say, 'I'm sorry', but the mobile phone was still smashed into pieces, and I had done it. I knew something was out of kilter here.

Here I was, a busy, energetic and apparently confident Christian leader, involved in a range of responsibilities and roles, with a good and loving home and family. I could tick most of the boxes of what I thought a man of my age might want to have achieved in life. I had, I believed, a solid, well-grounded Christian faith. In my view, I was managing to live my life reasonably well, according to the values and teachings of my faith. But when I stopped to think, as I did that night by the side of a quiet country lane in rural Cambridgeshire, then I knew that something was not right. I knew within myself a deep restlessness that my faith had never been able to address. I longed for rest and relief from the endless struggle to stay on top of everything. Sometimes, when I withdrew from my busy life for a brief while, I seemed to find some measure of peace and rest. But soon I was again back on the treadmill, back to rushing around, keeping on keeping on, making things happen and 'living life to the full'. I knew that somehow this was not enough. In fact, this way of life was itself the problem.

* * * * *

I love to travel. I have travelled in many parts of the world, in Africa, Europe and North America. Sometimes I would go to France or South Africa on holiday with the family, but I also liked to plan trips on my own, at times to wild and unexplored places. My wife would mostly tolerate my absences, and look after the family while I was away. It seemed to me that I needed the adventure of going to some place on the map 'just because it was there' and because I wanted to see what the place looked like. Once I travelled by train all the way to the northernmost station in Scotland, Thurso, just to enjoy the journey and then come back. I love the feeling of waking up in a hotel in a strange town or city, quietly enjoying the local breakfast, the smell of the coffee and the taste of the food. Then I will head out to watch, gaze and explore.

When I left South Africa and came to live in England, many new opportunities for travel opened up for me. I found that newspapers and magazines constantly offered advice and deals on exciting and interesting journeys and places to visit. There was a world of unlimited opportunity beckoning me. The only question was, 'How much can I fit into my busy life?'

I was particularly drawn to train journeys in Africa, Europe and North America. When I was growing up in South Africa, long, slow train journeys were a part of my life. Now I could spread my wings across the globe. One time, I booked tickets to fly to San Francisco and then take the train 2,000 miles to Chicago, where I would spend a couple of nights before continuing by train north to the Canadian border across North Dakota and Montana, then back to San Francisco. When we reached the Rocky Mountains, I planned to break my train journey in Whitefish, Montana, and drive up to Calgary in Canada to visit an old friend. This all went to plan, except that I had not realised how cold it can be high up in the Rocky Mountains in the middle of March. I found myself sitting alone in a rental car waiting to cross the Crowsnest pass from Fernie in British Columbia to Alberta in temperatures of minus 40°C. I was told that the pass had been closed because it was too dangerous.

I was about to book a room in a truck-stop motel near Fernie when I heard someone say, 'There is a convoy going through in half an hour. They say we can join the convoy if we are willing to take the risk.' I wanted to get to Calgary that night, so I didn't hesitate. As the convoy made its way slowly across the top of the mountain pass, with horizontal snow blowing across the road, I knew that I was on the edge, that things could very quickly go badly wrong here, but

I was also exhilarated. Okay, this was risky, but somehow this was being alive. This unforgettable experience was for me what living was all about.

But one year later, I discovered the downside of travel. I had planned to take my family back to South Africa for a holiday and time with family and friends. We would fly to Johannesburg and then drive to Kruger National Park for a week in the game reserve before continuing on to my family in KwaZulu-Natal. Everything was booked and paid for. Three days before we were due to travel, I became aware of a problem with my left eye. I went to see an optician, who sent me straight to the outpatients' clinic at the local hospital. An eye doctor examined my eyes and told me I could go ahead with my trip but that I should see a doctor again as soon as I returned to England. A week later, I woke up in a remote camp on the Mozambique border. A curtain of fluid seemed to have descended across my left eye. We managed to find a doctor in the game reserve, who said that I must go straight to the nearest eye clinic, in Nelspruit, just outside Kruger Park.

The doctor at the eye clinic took a quick look at my eye. 'You have a detached retina,' he said. 'You must have this operation today or you will lose the eye. Can you get to Johannesburg this afternoon?' Johannesburg was a three- or four-hour drive away. I looked at my family. My son John said, 'I'll drive, Dad. We can do it.'

The doctor phoned the Johannesburg Eye Hospital and made an appointment for me for emergency surgery later that afternoon. In the bright midday sun, we walked out into the clinic car park with some drinks and packets of sandwiches. John drove us without stopping four hours across the South African interior to Johannesburg, where a highly skilled surgeon was able to save my eye.

However, the nature of the surgery meant that it would be some months before I could see normally again, let alone drive a car or visit a game reserve. But we still had three weeks in South Africa.

I became a passenger, coping as best as I could behind my eye patch and my bewilderment. All I wanted was for us to go home, just to be safely back home where I could rest and recover.

It took some months and a further operation before I could obtain a new pair of glasses and was able to drive and read comfortably again. A detached retina is a serious medical emergency, as I now understand all too well. I guess I had hoped that things like this would not happen to me, and if they did, I would just deal with it. But life is not that simple.

Since this happened, my attitude to travel has begun to change. I read a quote from Malcolm Muggeridge, saying,

> When I look back on my life nowadays, which I sometimes do, what strikes me most forcibly about it is that what seemed at that time most significant and seductive, seems now most futile and absurd. For instance, success in all of its various guises; being known and being praised; ostensible pleasures, like acquiring money or seducing women, or travelling, going to and fro in the world and up and down in it like Satan, explaining and experiencing whatever Vanity Fair has to offer. In retrospect, all these exercises in self-gratification seem pure fantasy, what Pascal called, 'licking the earth'.[2]

I began to ask myself, 'Why do I want to visit all these places? Have I not seen enough of the world by now?' Never mind the weariness, the cost, the environmental footprint. For me, airports are not what they used to be. They used to be places of excitement with a sense of the privilege of air travel. Now they just seem to be long queues of people, endless shopping arcades, and more discomfort and waiting around. Maybe it is true that travel is a young person's game, but part of me does not want to get old. In my generation, we are told that 60 is the new 40 and 70 is the new 50. Or is it? What is going on here?

As I asked these questions, and others, I became aware that this was all tied up with the inner restlessness and driven activism that had been at the centre of my life for so long. These were questions that went deep into the heart of my own sense of identity, my sense of who I am and who I want to be seen to be. I was increasingly uncomfortable with the forces that were driving me. I knew that what I longed for was some greater measure of inner peace and contentment. But this is an elusive state of being about which most of us in contemporary western society can only dream.

In 2008 I was appointed to a new job, developing and running programmes and events in vocation and spirituality across a large area of southern England. I worked with two other Anglican clergy, Darrell Weyman and Sue Langdon, to set up some events for those in leadership and ministry, to be called 'The Contemplative Minister'. Darrell Weyman had read a great deal of the writing of Thomas Merton, the Trappist contemplative and writer. Darrell produced some notes to be handed out on the first Contemplative Minister day. On the front page, I read this quote from Thomas Merton:

> All sin starts from the assumption that my false self, the self that exists only in my own egocentric desires, is the fundamental reality of life to which everything else in the universe is ordered. Thus I use up my life in the desire for pleasures and the thirst for experiences, for power, honour, knowledge and love, to clothe this false self and construct its nothingness into something objectively real. And I wind experiences around myself and cover myself with pleasures and glory like bandages in order to make myself perceptible to myself and to the world, as if I were an invisible body that could only become visible when something visible covered its surface.[3]

As I read this, I could see that Merton had found a key to the inner struggle that I was experiencing. For Merton, a life devoted to what he calls the 'false self' is a life of sin. I needed to face up to the ways in which my own egocentric desires were running my life. I could see my own patterns of behaviour: the compulsions to keep acquiring more stuff and to be constantly achieving goals and completing tasks, and the need to indulge my appetites, particularly whenever I had nothing else with which to occupy myself. For me, the authority and power of the false self had never been seriously and consistently challenged. If I was ever to become my true self, and be true to my own heart, this had to change. This was not likely to be easy.

2

The pull of the ocean

When I was a boy, growing up in South Africa, I often went with my family to the beach on holiday. The Indian Ocean coast of KwaZulu-Natal is a mixture of long sandy beaches and large rocky outcrops. I spent many happy hours wandering over the rocks when the tide was low, looking for crabs, fish and shells in the rocky pools.

I also loved to swim in the ocean. But I learned when I was young that you must always respect the sea. The waves crashing in from the Indian Ocean can lift you up, turn you head over heels and thump you down on the sea floor with such force that you feel you have been through a gigantic washing machine. The currents can pull you along sometimes without you even realising what is happening until you suddenly find that you are some distance from where you thought you were, and possibly way out of your depth. Then you have to swim strongly back to where you know the place, to where you can still get back to the shore without difficulty.

The power of the ocean is a forceful reminder of the way in which our culture can pull and push us in ways that we may not even see happening. When I was young, the world seemed a simpler place. Maybe this is how life seems for every generation. It certainly is true for those who have lived through the technological changes of the past 60 years. I grew up in the culture of the 1950s and 1960s, mostly in rural South Africa. There was a lot of time to think, to play, to explore and to enjoy life. There was certainly little of the rush and the incessant buzz of information that we experience today. This was by no means a perfect world, but it was a world with few of today's gadgets and technology.

In our home on the farm where I grew up, there was no television. Computers were the stuff of science fiction. We had a radio and a battery-operated record player with a small collection of records. I grew up listening to *My Fair Lady* and *The Sound of Music* and very little else until I was given my first transistor radio. Our telephone was a party line, where you could speak freely to any of the twelve or so local farming people who were connected on our line. The problem was that anyone else on the line could listen in at any time. You could also only make one call at a time on this line, so if someone else was having a long conversation, you just had to wait. Making a trunk call outside of our local area was a matter of placing the call with the exchange, and then waiting for them to call you back. Sometimes this could mean waiting for hours for a trunk call to come through.

This was the age of telegrams and photograph albums, of board games and writing letters and collecting postage stamps. The generation that is growing up as I write this will think of many of these as strange old customs from a previous age. Memory, of course, charges this with a soft patina of nostalgia and comfort. Looking back to childhood there is bound to be a sense of wistful longing for much that is now lost. We travel so far from all that once was familiar, from things and people that once we knew and loved, and, of course, we can never go back. That world is gone forever.

So maybe the world of the 21st century is not a worse or a better world. But it undoubtedly presents significant challenges for all those who cherish a life of rest and quietness, contentment and kindness.

* * * * *

There are many ways to describe the age of electronic media and information technology. This is the age of the internet, the digital age, the age of acceleration, where everything happens faster and faster. Either we keep up or we will be left behind. There are computers, 24-hour news and fast food; people are even walking faster. Technology is constantly driving this accelerated pace of life. Computers are getting faster. It is widely recognised that processing power tends to double every two years. But where will this end? Where is this taking us?

There is no doubt that this rapid development of technology is changing the way we live. Some will say that our lives are getting better and better. Robert Colvile has written a book entitled *The Great Acceleration: How the world is getting faster, faster* (Bloomsbury, 2016). He maintains that 'a high pace of life is generally associated with happiness, prosperity and fulfilment'.[4] In his view, the benefits of the age of acceleration outweigh the downsides, provided we discipline ourselves to slow down and switch off when we need to.

There are great benefits to digital technology. We have access to vast quantities of information for which not long ago we would have had to go trawling through encyclopedias and libraries. I appreciate instant access to cricket scores and hotel bookings, to road traffic reports and train times. I do not want to be left behind by technology. Indeed, I suspect that I cannot afford to be.

The internet also provides a platform for accountability like never before. Politicians, leaders and public figures are subject to a new level of scrutiny. People are getting caught out cheating on their taxes, on their spouses and on their employers. This is bad news for some people, but good news for many others. There is much about the internet that is positive and that has changed many people's lives for the better.

But Colvile recognises the effect of the information age on our society:

> Human beings are social creatures. We do not live at our own pace: we adjust to the rhythms of others. And those rhythms are speeding up. Compared with the early 1990s, walking

speeds across the world have increased by at least 10%. We are talking more quickly, acting more quickly, growing ever less tolerant of dither and delay. So if you ever get the feeling that life is speeding up, that events and trends and demands are coming thicker and faster – that is exactly what is happening.[5]

This has significant implications for those of us for whom the spiritual centre of our lives is essential to who we are and what we do. We are increasingly faced with a way of life where, seven days a week, events and trends and demands are confronting us at every turn. We seem to be constantly engaged, dealing with stuff. A lot of this adrenalin-fuelled activity can be exciting and attractive, particularly when we are young and have energy to burn. But it can also be exhausting. The principle of sabbath rest has surely never been more relevant than it is right now.

So we are, as a society, becoming busier and busier, and moving faster and faster. There are so many things to do, so many opportunities to be grasped, so many goals to be achieved. The number of people in the UK who regularly work more than 48 hours a week has gone up in the last decade to almost 3.5 million, according to a recent Trades Union Congress report, which adds, 'Regularly working more than 48 hours per week is linked to a significantly increased risk of developing heart disease, stress, mental illness, strokes and diabetes.'[6]

In my own work in the Church of England, I have come across many ordained ministers who routinely work 60 hours a week or more. In some diocesan appointments, this is considered normal, because there is no other way to handle the workload. The digital age does not seem to have given us more free time or made us more creative in our work lives. If anything, volumes of emails and online information are a constant blight on our working lives. We may come back to the office after a week's holiday to be faced with 500 or more emails. Not all are important, but they all have to be sifted through. Surely there was something to be said for sitting down and opening a small pile of letters, giving each one some thought, and then carefully replying to each with a hand-written note. But those days are long gone for most of us.

Part of the stress of modern life results from information overload. The sheer volume of information that confronts us daily is impossible to absorb or process fully. So we live with an awareness that we may somewhere have missed something important. We know there is always more that we could be doing, or reading, or checking. We make our to-do lists and try to clear the emails and the tasks, but there's always more. We have to deal with the fact that we can only absorb so much information in one day.

This is the age of excess. If we live in the developed western world, the chances are that we already have too many clothes, too many gadgets and appliances, and too much entertainment available for us to ever take it all in. There is choice everywhere, a vast array of options and alternatives online, in the supermarket, on the screen and in the world of leisure activities. Choice seems to me like a luxury, and yet it has become the norm. Most of the time, I would prefer less choice and more quality. But again, I suspect that those days are gone.

In 2010 Nicholas Carr raised the important issue of how the internet is affecting our brains. His book is called *The Shallows: How the internet is changing the way we think, read and remember*. In a related article, Carr writes:

> I'm not thinking the way I used to think. I feel it most strongly when I'm reading. I used to find it easy to immerse myself in a book or lengthy article. My mind would get caught up in the twists of the narrative or the turns of the argument and I'd spend hours strolling through long stretches of prose. That's rarely the case anymore. Now the concentration starts to drift after a page or two. I get fidgety, lose the thread, begin looking for something else to do. I feel as though I'm always dragging

my wayward brain back to the text. The deep reading that used to come naturally has become a struggle.[7]

Carr believes that our dependence on the internet is making us shallow, and that we are becoming increasingly unreflective and superficial in many of our judgements. There is a movement away from depth, from profound reflection and wrestling with ambiguity. We see the effects of this now wherever we look in our politics and our social discourse. Social media is awash with comment and abuse that cuts out proper discussion and reflection, and resorts instead to immediate reaction and dismissal. This is both a challenge and a concern for any of those who seek to be attentive to the heart of God for his world. The psalms say, 'Deep calls to deep' (42:7), and, 'O Lord! Your thoughts are very deep!' (92:5). The Bible calls us again and again to align our thoughts and behaviour with the ways of the Lord, not to be tossed to and fro and blown about with every new idea and scheme.

For Carr, the internet is not just part of our culture, in the way that the telephone, radio or TV became part of our culture. He sees that the internet is:

becoming the whole of our culture, it's becoming our map, our telephone, our calculator, our source of news and entertainment and our shopping mall. We carry it around in our pockets, 24/7. When we talk to each other, we're holding it, glancing at it, worrying about it. And it's been around for only the blink of an eye. What defines the internet? It's a machine for distracting you. That's its business model.[8]

We are liable to be constantly distracted by our smartphones and our devices. Even in the middle of a social gathering, a meeting or a conversation, we look at our phones and screens to see what is happening or who is messaging us. For a while I was in the habit of having my little device by my bed at night. Soon I was checking my emails and messages before I even got out of bed in the morning.

I quickly realised that this was not good for me or my stress levels. Boundaries must be put in place in order to live a productive and disciplined life. Our devices need to be taught this lesson, but it is not easy for many of us to do this.

It seems to me that it is necessary to be deliberate and intentional about our use of digital technology and about how we avoid multiplying these distractions. Do I really need a smartphone? Do I need to be part of social networks, such as Facebook, Twitter and Instagram? After careful consideration, I recently decided to remove myself from all social networks. I had joined Facebook some years ago, having been invited by a friend who I trusted and respected. I wanted to see what Facebook was like and how I could benefit from being in touch with people who otherwise I would not be able to contact. I quickly found a large group of friends, some of whom I had not seen or heard from for many years. A few of my friends posted prolifically, with comments and photographs and snippets of news. Most of my friends did not use Facebook much at all. Maybe this says something about my generation, who did not grow up with social media and for whom it is not instinctive to use. But eventually I decided that I did not need the nonsense, the adverts and the trivia and, with some difficulty, I managed to delete my Facebook page.

For many people social media becomes an addiction. We may find ourselves checking our phones many times, even within one hour, to see if there are messages from our friends. Smartphone apps offer so many potentially addictive possibilities. Online gambling is one of these, but many are more subtle. I had a lot of fun playing a motor-racing game that is available as a free app on my tablet. Initially it was straightforward, with a series of races on imaginary tracks and remarkably real cars. But soon things changed. I found that I had to start earning online money and gold to buy and upgrade new cars. I had to play every day or I would be penalised, and I was always being tempted with the possibility of buying better cars and upgrades with real money. This game, like many others, can become seriously addictive.

So we find ourselves immersed in a world where we are constantly distracted and also, if we are not careful, constantly being tracked or watched. The internet now functions as a vast surveillance apparatus, which works ceaselessly to control and direct our desires and appetites. It is immensely powerful and is changing the world, even as I write these words.

This is the culture that surrounds us, the ocean in which we swim. If we do not want to be simply pulled along by the current, and soon find ourselves completely out of our depth, we must be very careful. Like the sea, we need to treat this prevailing culture with great respect. This does not mean that we cannot go swimming at all. But we have to know where the currents are too strong for us, and what is necessary for our safety and survival. Go swimming in the Indian Ocean, but do not go too far from the shore, and always be ready to get out quickly when the sea gets too rough. The shoreline is the place we know, where we can stand firm and be strong. For Christians, our strength is in the Lord our God. He is our lifeline, our Saviour, our help and our refuge in time of need. We must take great care not to be so caught up in all that is offered by the culture of our age that we lose the foundation on which our lives depend.

3

The real God

In September 1969 I was a first-year undergraduate student at the University of Natal in Pietermaritzburg, South Africa. I had joined a number of student societies and organisations, including NUX (the student newspaper) and UCM (the University Christian Movement). I was young and keen to discover what the world of university life had to offer. I was invited to attend a weekend Formation School run by UCM at a Roman Catholic retreat and conference centre called Redacres, near Pietermaritzburg. We met together with other students from various colleges and university campuses. As a white South African, this was my first-ever experience of a non-racial residential event. Among those attending was a small group from the black medical school in Durban, known then as UNNE (University of Natal non-European). The students who were there from UNNE were Aletta and Steve, together with Siepo from Johannesburg. I enjoyed the weekend and soon became a member of the local UCM committee.

The following year, in July 1970, I attended the National UCM conference, Encounter 70, at Wilgespruit near Johannesburg. By this time, the ideas of people like Steve and some of the other UCM leaders were becoming much more well-known and controversial. At Encounter 70 there was a long theological discussion on the subject 'God – white or black?' The conference report tells the story:

Many blacks argued that Christianity was becoming increasingly irrelevant to black people in South Africa. In fact, more sinister than irrelevant. Christianity that the black people had come to accept was almost entirely the interpretation which had been placed on it by whites. And this was not simply a reference to the missionaries of the past. The seminary training given to black clerics was almost entirely in the hands of the whites. These whites could not but place their perspectives on what they taught. These perspectives could not be divorced from their social position and self-interest. Consequently the Christianity accepted by blacks was a Christianity biased in favour of whites.[9]

At the centre of the discussion was the question of who God is. Is the real God white or black? Clearly our culture and society determine to some extent our understanding of the nature of God. I came to realise that the God of white South African Christians was not a God that the black students at UCM recognised. During this time in South Africa, I was witnessing first-hand the emergence of Black Theology and the Black Consciousness movement. The outstanding leader in this new movement was the young black student who I had met at the Formation School. He was Steve Biko.

At the Formation School in 1969, I had been impressed by Steve Biko. He was articulate and charismatic. Although I was young and had little idea of the background to Black Theology and its implications, I was learning quickly. Steve was clearly a leader, a man who was ahead of his time. This led me to a significant level of involvement both in UCM and also in student politics, as I became the editor of the student newspaper on our campus. By 1971 many of us in the UCM were being harassed and intimidated by the Security Police. Most of the leaders of UCM were given five-year banning orders, and the UCM had itself collapsed by mid-1972. It would have been a lot easier for a young white Christian student to avoid these issues, and simply to enjoy student life and concentrate on my degree. A number of my student friends warned me that I was looking for trouble. My parents wanted me to have nothing to do with the University Christian Movement.

This for me was a time of exploration and adventure. I was willing to go wherever I was led by my search for God, for truth and for the hope for the future of my country. My experience of UCM and some other student organisations had given me a new vision for the future of South Africa. This is a vision of society based not on race but on our common humanity in God's sight. I knew without any shadow of doubt that all South Africans, of whatever race, language, religion or gender, were equally made in God's image and equally precious in his sight. But not all Christians in South Africa felt this way.

I remember going to a Bible study group in my university residence. Some of the students came from remote rural areas and their views on South African politics were conservative and defensive. I remember one student explaining to me that the Bible's teaching says that God created the white race to be the leaders and masters in society, and the black races were created to be servants. It seems extraordinary now, but this is what he believed to be biblical truth. I asked him to show me a passage in the Bible that supported this. He turned to Genesis 9:25, where Noah says to his son Ham, 'Cursed be Canaan; lowest of slaves shall he be to his brothers.' He then turned to Joshua 9:22–23: 'Joshua summoned [the Canaanites], and said to them, "Why did you deceive us, saying, 'We are very far from you', while in fact you are living among us? Now therefore you are cursed, and some of you shall always be slaves, hewers of wood and drawers of water for the house of my God."'

The explanation I was given was that the sons and daughters of Ham were the black races, and these were decreed in the Bible to be 'hewers of wood and drawers of water' for the people of God. I didn't accept a word of this, but I was amazed and concerned that this kind of teaching could be believed in all sincerity by a Christian student at the University of Natal. His views would not have been widely held among students at Natal University at that time, but many would have agreed that blacks and whites should not mix socially or professionally as equals.

I soon realised that there were complex problems in understanding the nature of God and the interpretation of the Bible among white

South African Christians. I was often told that Romans 13 teaches that we must all obey the governing authorities and that therefore the church must stay out of politics. In many white congregations at that time, there would be a lot of trouble if apartheid was discussed or even mentioned from the pulpit. It seemed to me that many white Christians wanted only to worship a God who had nothing to say about justice, apartheid or the suffering of black people. But this surely was not the real God.

An important question for each one of us living in the distracted culture of the 21st century is this: which God or gods do I choose to serve? As Bob Dylan famously said, 'You gotta serve somebody.' We may say that we are serving God, but there are many false gods that clamour for our allegiance and attention. We all worship something or someone.

How do we find the real God? This is not nearly as simple as it may seem. My South African experience has left me aware that I need to be alert to the ways in which my culture and my own preferences could be distorting my understanding of God and God's will. None of us can fully know God as he or she is. As the psalmist says,

> Bless the Lord, O my soul.
>   O Lord my God, you are very great.
> PSALM 104:1

> O Lord, you have searched me and known me.
> You know when I sit down and when I rise up;
>   you discern my thoughts from far away...
> Such knowledge is too wonderful for me;
>   it is so high that I cannot attain it.
> PSALM 139:1–2, 6

The God of the Old and New Testaments is the creator of all, the source of life, the one who is himself beyond time and space. We cannot with our finite human minds comprehend the infinite mystery of Almighty God. Yet the Bible says that we can know God, we can cry out to him, we can seek his face. God has created us for himself, and he longs for us to know his love and care for us, and to walk with him. Above all we can, and should, worship God because of who he is, because of his greatness and majesty and power, and also because of his mercy and his unfailing love for us.

Christians believe that the real God is the God who is revealed in the pages of the Bible, the God of our Lord Jesus Christ. He is God who can be known and loved, because his very nature is love. And yet this God remains shrouded in mystery. He is God alone, immortal, invisible, God only wise.

There is a dilemma that faces many, if not all, of those who choose to believe in this God: why does God allow his children to suffer? How can a loving God look at the civil war in Syria or the famine and suffering in South Sudan and not intervene? Why, O God, why? How can an all-powerful God not turn the path of a hurricane away from a small Caribbean island? Why do such disasters happen to people who are already poor and without the means to protect themselves properly?

I have thought and read a great deal about this, and I do not know the answer. I have seen things happen in South Africa that have left me profoundly shaken and saddened. I do not know why the world that God has made and that he loves is a place in which such terrible things can and do happen. But at the end of the day, I am faced with a simple choice: do I continue to believe in this God whose love and mercy I have known in so many ways, or do I choose to say that there is no God, and decide to live without him? It seems to me to be a choice between mystery or atheism. The mystery is sometimes bewildering and often baffling, but for me it contains a depth of truth alongside which atheism is but a dim shadow.

The fact is that we do not and cannot understand God's ways:

For my thoughts are not your thoughts,
nor are your ways my ways, says the Lord.
For as the heavens are higher than the earth,
so are my ways higher than your ways
and my thoughts than your thoughts.
ISAIAH 55:8–9

It does seem that inevitably we will all face suffering in some form, and our faith will be tested. Sometimes these tests and trials may be severe, and some of us will lose our faith altogether. For others, the test of our faith leads to it being deepened and refined. Some of what we have believed may be shown to be an inadequate, or even a false, understanding of the real God who is not merely a projection of our own ideas and desires. We may have to wrestle long and hard before we are willing to let go of that which is not compatible with our experience and understanding of the real God.

Jesus teaches us that the Holy Spirit is 'the Spirit of truth', and his work is to guide us into all truth (John 16:13). Most importantly, perhaps, it is the work of the Holy Spirit to lead us to the real God, to the truth about God. He makes Jesus known to us, and so leads us to the love of our heavenly Father. Jesus says, 'He will glorify me, because he will take what is mine and declare it to you. All that the Father has is mine. For this reason I said that he will take what is mine and declare it to you' (John 16:14–15).

The work of the Holy Spirit is to draw us day by day to know and serve the real God. We may find that we have been serving other gods even while we had, as we thought, committed our lives to the real God. Obedience to Jesus Christ as Lord and Saviour is not straightforward. These other gods may take many names and forms. Ambition, self-indulgence and overwork are common these days. Many of us are, to a greater or lesser degree, possessed by our possessions. The pursuit of success and prosperity can easily become part of our religion. Sometimes our doctrines and our views about political and economic matters may need to be carefully reconsidered as we grow more deeply into the truth of God's love revealed in Jesus Christ. Our culture and the pressures of our society may condition us and conform us to a pattern of life that is not conducive to holy living.

How then do we find the real God? The Christian faith is rooted in revelation that has been tested and relied upon for thousands of years. We have the Bible, in which the ways of God are made known to us, sometimes in all their perplexing mystery. I don't claim to understand God, but I have experienced enough of his truth, goodness and love to believe and to know that the Bible tells me the truth about who God is and about who I am. I know that my life is in his hands, come what may. For me it is true that, in the words of a song I learnt as a child, 'Jesus loves me, this I know, for the Bible tells me so.'

For Christians, God has revealed himself in many ways in scripture and in the natural world, but above all God has made himself known in Jesus (Hebrews 1:1–3). Jesus is God in human form, God the Son. 'He is the image of the invisible God' (Colossians 1:15). If you have seen Jesus, you have seen God. As I read and study the words of the four gospels, I find myself asking, 'Where did all this come from if not from God?' I know that in the life and teaching of Jesus Christ, I find the truth about God for which my heart is longing. In him alone I find my peace, my rest, my way.

But I am also aware that I am surrounded by pressures and temptations that may lead me to serve other gods, even as I think that I am following Christ. I am being pushed and pulled continually by the ocean of my culture and by my own desires and ambitions. I am at the same time being led by the Holy Spirit to desire and search for the true God, who loves me as I am. I know that in seeking him, I will find him, because that is his promise to me (Matthew 7:7), and in finding him, I will also find rest for my soul (Matthew 11:29). This is the fruit of a relationship with the real God.

Part Two

The false self: the compulsions and the remedies

4

Discovering the false self

Rutland is the smallest county in England. Its motto, *Multum in parvo*, is Latin for 'Much in little'. That is my own experience of Rutland. The county town, Oakham, is about ten minutes' drive from where I now live. This is a beautiful part of England – quiet, unassuming, friendly.

At the heart of Oakham is Oakham School, founded in 1584 by Archdeacon Robert Johnson. Thomas Merton was a pupil at Oakham School from 1929 to 1933, during which time he became joint editor of the school magazine, the *Oakhamian*. Merton writes:

> In the autumn of 1929 I went to Oakham. There was something very pleasant and peaceful about the atmosphere of this little market town, with its school and its old 14th-century church with the grey spire, rising in the middle of a wide Midland vale.[10]

In the Oakham School library there is a special collection of books and papers of particular importance to the school, including a whole section devoted to Merton. In recent months, I have regularly gone to the library in Oakham to sit and read and reflect on the life and teaching of Thomas Merton. Somehow being in this place, off the beaten track, quiet and sheltered, seems to draw me close to the heart and wisdom of one of the great contemplative thinkers and writers of our time.

Merton died in 1968, but his influence on Christian spirituality over the years has been incalculable. Merton called the Christian church back to its contemplative roots. In recent times we have seen the emergence of fresh streams of contemplative church and new monasticism. Much of this can be traced back to Thomas Merton.

Merton wrote at the beginning of his great book *New Seeds of Contemplation*, first published in 1961:

> Contemplation is the highest expression of man's intellectual and spiritual life. It is that life itself, fully awake, fully active, fully aware that it is alive. It is spiritual wonder. It is spontaneous awe at the sacredness of life, of being. It is gratitude for life, for awareness and for being. It is a vivid realization of the fact that life and being in us proceed from an invisible, transcendent and infinitely abundant Source. Contemplation is, above all, awareness of the reality of that Source.[11]

Contemplation, says Merton, leads us to the real God.

In coming to know the real God, we respond to a call from God to become our true selves in order that we may freely love God as those who are completely and unconditionally loved by him. In *New Seeds of Contemplation*, Merton goes on to write about the need to recognise the false self in each of us, in order that we may know the reality of the one who is the infinitely abundant source of life. Merton writes:

> There is no evil in anything created by God, nor can anything of his become an obstacle to our union in him. The obstacle is in our 'self', that is to say in the tenacious need to maintain our separate, external, egotistic will. It is when we refer all things to this outward and false 'self' that we alienate ourselves from reality and from God. It is then the false self that is our god, and we love everything for the sake of this self.[12]

The false self is essentially about 'me'. When I am at the centre of everything, when I am in control of everything, the false self is in charge. The truth is that I am never at the centre of everything, or in control of everything. That position belongs to God alone. It all goes back to the garden of Eden. The temptation that Adam and Eve faced, and yielded to, was to eat the forbidden fruit, and so to become like God. 'The serpent said to the woman, "You will not die;

for God knows that when you eat of it your eyes will be opened, and you will be like God, knowing good and evil'" (Genesis 3:4–5).

The false self wants me to be like God. It wants the world to revolve around me and my needs and my wants. My life is then first and foremost about me, not about God. When I am most concerned about what other people are thinking of me or how I am being portrayed, or even misrepresented, the false self is kicking in. We do of course often feel the effect of other people's opinions and judgements about us and about what we have said or done. We may feel elated, or we may feel bruised. But if God is at the centre, we will know, deep within ourselves, that the praise or the hurt that we feel is not the ultimate truth about us. The ultimate truth is that we are loved unconditionally by God.

Merton says, 'For me to be a saint means to be myself. Therefore the problem of sanctity and salvation is in fact the problem of finding out who I am and of discovering my true self.'[13] My daily life is a continual movement from true self to false self, and then back to the true self. The false self usually governs my first response to the things that happen to me. It is my default position. This is how my daily life unfolds, because my false self is part of who I am. But I am learning to believe that God loves me as I am, and that at all times and in every circumstance he looks upon me with unfailing compassion and goodness. I am his beloved child. So when I respond to events with self-pity, self-interest or self-importance, God is not surprised. He knows that this is who I am. He is my Father. His love calls out to me, again and again, leading me away from a 'me-first' response towards a 'Jesus-first' response. God reaches out to me in compassion and never in condemnation. 'There is therefore now no condemnation for those who are in Christ Jesus. For the law of the Spirit of life in Christ Jesus has set you free from the law of sin and of death' (Romans 8:1–2).

It takes a long time to learn to live from the still centre where God's love holds me secure in my identity as his beloved child. The false self is always there, and when I am busy and the pressure is on, the false self has a great chance to run the show for a while. This is why, for all those who are seeking to live from the still centre, daily prayer is essential. We need to keep coming back to the place where we stop our busyness and return to the one who always loves and receives us. This was Jesus' own practice. He would leave the crowds and all the demands of the people and withdraw to a deserted place to pray. This was not something that Jesus occasionally found time to do. It seems to have been his regular, probably daily, practice and discipline (see Matthew 14:23; Luke 4:42, 5:16, 9:28; Mark 6:46, 9:2; John 8:1).

I find that it is important for me to build into my life wherever possible regular times during the day and evening to stop and be quiet before God. The morning is my main time for prayer, both contemplative and intercessory. I try to stop before lunch for at least five minutes of quiet prayer. In South Africa during the 1980s, we would aim to stop whatever we were doing at noon each day to be quiet for a few minutes and then to say the prayer for Africa:

God, bless Africa
guard her children
guide her leaders
and give her peace for Jesus Christ's sake.[14]

Through this discipline I have learned the value of stopping, even in the middle of a busy day, and returning to the centre, even for just a few minutes of quietness. Later in the afternoon I aim to stop work or whatever I am doing at five o'clock to be quiet and reflect upon my day. Then I will say a short office of evening prayer. Lastly, before I go to sleep I aim to take at least a few minutes to reflect, to give thanks and to pray.

This pattern usually works well for me in normal daily living. When I am away on retreat I have much greater opportunity to root my whole life in prayer, particularly if I am staying in a monastery or religious community. But in a normal busy life a deeper level of disciplined withdrawal does not seem possible, or at least for me. It seems that God is drawing me by gentle encouragement to find practical ways to live each day closer to him and more in tune with his presence. Being hard on myself about this is not likely to be helpful.

In all this, I am seeking to return to my true self, to the place within my own heart where I am closest to God. This is a journey in which finding my true self and knowing the real God are synonymous. You cannot have one without the other. Merton writes, 'If I find him, I will find myself, and if I find my true self I will find him.'[15] As I travel further on this road, I realise more and more that my false self is continually trying to throw me off course. Sometimes it is a major battle simply to stop what I am doing or thinking about and to physically go to the place of prayer, the place of being still. My false self seems to be willing to do just about anything to keep me occupied with my own thoughts and ideas. There is a surrender that is required, a handing over of control that my false self sometimes finds very difficult.

To let go of the demands of the false self is to return to the one in whom I find true freedom. The false self seems to manifest itself in my desires for security and safety, for power and control and for esteem and significance. As I pray, I may need to let go of one or more of these desires. I then consciously try to let God be God in me at that moment. This is a handing over, a surrender, in which all my attempts to sort out my situation or my problems are given over in trust to my loving heavenly Father: 'Now it's up to you, Lord. It is in your hands.'

As we grow in the daily practice of returning to the true self and to the God who loves us as we are, we find a rippling effect that increasingly touches every part of life. As the centre becomes clearer and stronger, even the shadows and obstacles in the dark corners of our lives will begin to be disturbed. This is how contemplative practice transforms us. As we engage the true self, the false self will be more and more exposed. We will find out with fresh insight how some of our habits and patterns of life are hindering us in deepening our relationship with the real God.

In the gospels of Matthew and Luke there are accounts of the temptation of Jesus in the wilderness (Matthew 4:1–11; Luke 4:1–13). Jesus was tempted to turn stones into bread because he was hungry. The temptation before him was to put the security of physical provision for his personal needs before his obedience to God. Then Jesus was tempted to throw himself from the pinnacle of the temple, and to put God to the test to see if God would indeed send his angels to save him. Jesus' response was that we are not to put God to the test. We are to humbly trust God in all our circumstances. It is not for us to presume upon God and tell him what to do, as though he were our servant. We are not in control. Our lives are in his hands.

Lastly, Jesus was tempted by Satan to fall down and worship him, in order that Jesus might be given by Satan all the kingdoms of the world and their glory. Jesus' response was again from scripture: 'It is written, "Worship the Lord your God, and serve only him"' (Matthew 4:10). Glory and honour belong to God; he alone is worthy of our worship. When we seek glory and significance for ourselves, we are again putting ourselves instead of God at the centre. The way of Jesus is the way of servanthood, humility and hiddenness. The way of Jesus leads to the cross not the crown.

The false self is preoccupied with the desires for security and safety, power and control, and esteem and significance. These are areas where each of us can easily be led into temptation. The sin does not lie in being tempted; Jesus was tempted in each of these areas and stood firm. It is important to note that on each occasion, Jesus used the truth about God as revealed in scripture to turn away temptation. Satan placed before Jesus the suggestion of a sinful action. Jesus could have done the wrong deed and entered into sin. On each occasion, he resisted and remained obedient to the Father.

We too will be tested on this path. The desires of the false self, the 'me-first' part of who we are, provide a continual opportunity for us to be drawn into actions that can be both sinful and damaging in all sorts of ways. In our culture, we are being constantly offered incentives and opportunities for the ways of the false self to rule our behaviour. When I am alone or tired or under pressure, I find that I am particularly vulnerable to these temptations. I may resort to different patterns of behaviour: to go shopping and acquire some more things; to work a bit harder and feel a sense of achievement; or to indulge myself, perhaps with a big bar of chocolate or some junk TV. All this may seem harmless and innocuous and surely not sinful.

But what is actually going on here? The compulsions of the false self are at work through my own inclinations to acquire, achieve and indulge. Some achieving in life is healthy and necessary. Surely, we should be free to buy and consume what we need for daily life. God's gifts are given to be enjoyed and celebrated. But there is a shadow to our achieving, our acquiring and our indulging, especially in contemporary culture. The call to become our true selves in the service of Jesus Christ will make inescapable the need for us to confront this shadow.

5

Acquire

I was walking down the street in a beautiful English cathedral city. Among the shops and restaurants was an upmarket estate agency offering homes and properties in attractive villages and desirable locations. A small display of glossy magazines caught my eye. The magazine was called *Acquire*.

This seems to me to tell the story of life for many people in our society. It's all about the opportunities that are placed before us each day to acquire. Acquiring is widely understood to give meaning and purpose to our lives. There are so many wonderful things for us to acquire. All we need is the money and the desire.

The age of excess confronts us at every turn. For those of us who inhabit the western consumerist economies, we are surrounded by too much of everything. That is not to say that everyone has enough. If only that were true, we could perhaps feel more comfortable with the way our societies are ordered. But the world of globalisation and consumerism is also a world of ever-growing inequality. The rich are getting richer, and in many places the poor are getting poorer. Some of us have more than enough stuff, far more than we can use, while others of us do not have enough to provide even the basic necessities of life.

Having spent most of my life in Africa, I am acutely aware of some of the ways in which the demands and needs of British society are being supplied and supported by global imbalances and inequalities. What you can acquire these days depends very much on where you live. A nurse in South Africa currently earns an average yearly salary of R212,560 (South African rand).[16] This is equivalent to around

£11,800 (British pounds), or just under £1,000 per month. A nurse in Zambia earns around 477 kwacha (or around £400) per month.[17] On the other hand, the average salary for a registered nurse in the UK is now £23,491,[18] which is just under £2,000 per month. Nurses in Britain are not regarded as being well paid and in many parts of the country will struggle to afford to pay a mortgage, or even to pay the rent on this salary.

Clearly there are major imbalances at work here. The cost of living varies enormously from place to place, but even in Zambia the cost of feeding, clothing and housing a family is considerable. It is not difficult to see why, for some years now, countries like South Africa and Zambia have been suffering a brain drain, where health workers and other skilled people are drawn to migrate to more developed countries. Even though housing is much cheaper in Zambia than it is in Britain, there are still significant costs if you want to buy and maintain a home, car, computer and smartphone. So health workers and other skilled people, and young people especially, are drawn to move to countries where they can earn far more money. Low salaries and poor working conditions are usually the main drivers of this migration. But the result is that the health service in Britain is increasingly staffed by those from developing countries who have been recruited with offers of higher salaries and better lifestyles. The cost for countries like Zambia, South Africa and many others is a depleted and diminished health service, where the need for good primary healthcare is urgent, and in many cases desperate.

Our culture of excess, of choice and luxury, is not without cost to others. We depend upon labour, raw materials and manufactured goods that are sourced in countries where wages and standards of living are far lower than our own. This alone ought to make us ask some hard questions. But the culture of consumerism is seductive. When this is the world we inhabit, we easily make assumptions about what we think we should have, even about what we are entitled to. 'In the affluent society no useful distinction can be made between luxuries and necessities,' wrote J.K. Galbraith in *The Affluent*

Society in 1958.[19] The problem with the affluent consumer-centred society is that we lose the ability to distinguish between what we need and what we want. Greed can be a subtle sin, especially when all around us greed is being marketed and clothed with a veneer of acceptability. The Christian church has long recognised greed as sinful, as a serious obstacle to knowing and following Christ. Greed is indeed one of the seven deadly sins.

The Dictionary of Christian Spirituality defines greed as:

> the inordinate love of material things and, by extension, of power, position and anything else that can be obtained. It is not the 'having' or 'wanting' that is always wrong, but the selfish or hedonistic motives, unjust means and misplaced trust that make such pursuits wrong.[20]

Greed is the desire to always want more of something, so that one is never satisfied, never content.

It is not straightforward to distinguish between what someone needs and what is too much. We are all different, and what is enough for one person may not be enough for someone else. We each need to look at our own motives, at the state of our hearts, to discern where our desires are coming from and who it is that we are seeking to please and serve. Ultimately, this is about whether we are serving God or serving our 'me-first' false self. It is also a matter of knowing where our true and deepest security lies. In whom and what do we put our trust, for the future and for our present joy, comfort and well-being? And then there is the issue of unjust means. Who is being exploited or neglected in order that we may have what we want?

Jesus spoke a number of times about treasure. Treasure is more than a beautiful old chest full of precious stones, gold and silver coins, bracelets and ornaments. Treasure is what we love and value most highly. If we treasure something, we cherish or place great value on it, even if it is not an expensive or valuable object. Treasure is anything to which we give time, effort and energy to obtain and to keep. Jesus said, 'Where your treasure is, there your heart will be also' (Matthew 6:21).

As ever, Jesus is most interested in what is happening in our hearts. He is saying that if we want to know where our heart's true allegiance lies, we should ask ourselves to identify those things to which we devote most of our time and energy. What occupies our thoughts when we are alone, not in public view, not telling others what we perhaps would want them to hear about us? Why is it that too often when I get home after a long day's work, I find myself spending an hour or so on my computer or tablet browsing the internet, looking at new CDs or books that I might order online, or checking out used car websites for particular high-performance cars?

I suspect that this is my false self at work. And I am not too concerned as long as I know that this side of me is not going to have the last word. I do like fast cars, crime novels and rock music. But they are not my gods. My God will, I pray, have the last word on how I live and how I choose to spend my money. My heart's desire is to honour him.

Jesus says, 'Do not store up for yourselves treasures on earth, where moth and rust consume and where thieves break in and steal; but store up for yourselves treasures in heaven, where neither moth nor rust consumes and where thieves do not break in and steal' (Matthew 6:19–20). Jesus is very specific in his teaching about the choice that his followers have to face: 'You cannot serve God and wealth [Greek: *mammon*]' (Matthew 6:24).

The Archbishop of Canterbury, Justin Welby, has spoken of 'the tensions that arise in our society because we are so dominated by economics and finance, the modern aliases of Mammon'. Welby says, 'It is difficult to live well and with right attitudes in a society where the current prevailing values push us in a very different direction.'[21] The economic model that our society has adopted is inseparably bound to the imperative value of consumption. It is consumerism and consumption that drive economic growth. Growth is important for the creation of jobs and for the improvement of standards of living, but the downside is that consumption has also become the primary focus of much of modern life. Alan Storkey says that consumption 'is the chief rival to God in our culture'. He writes:

> The faith lives and grows as myth because it has countless well-paid servants who, though often unhappy, go about their Master's business. The servants of the Lord God are dwarfed in number and working hours by the servants of consumption. Its ability to recruit seems unlimited.[22]

The pressure and compulsion to acquire is integral to life in a consumerist society. For all Christians, and especially for those in Christian leadership, this presents a significant challenge. This is about our discipleship, but this is also, more seriously, about our ultimate allegiance. Who do I serve? Who or what am I worshipping? What is it that rules my heart? We have to guard our hearts very carefully when faced with such a powerful and persuasive alternative to our God. Christian leaders are called to be those who show the way. We are those who by our lives and not just our words are to reveal what holy living looks like in our age and culture. If we fail in this, we fail before God in our vocation as leaders.

Consumerism and the compulsion to acquire raise important questions about our relationship with God. Jesus said the first and greatest commandment is this: 'You shall love the Lord your God with all your heart, and with all your soul, and with all your mind' (Matthew 22:37). And he said that the second is like it: 'You shall love your neighbour as yourself' (Matthew 22:39). The two are inseparably bound together. This is about our love for God, and this is also about our love and care for our neighbour, locally and globally, as well as our love and care for ourselves.

Roger Moore, the former James Bond actor, was asked, as he approached his 90th birthday, for his advice on 'How to be a man'.

Among his reply to *The Sunday Times Style* magazine was this:

> Always Question Yourself. You have to say, 'Am I making the world a better place? Am I making this a better moment? Is this the right thing to do?' That's the start of being a man. To question yourself, to question an action – and a reaction.

He went on to say:

> The ideal gift a man should get a woman is... You have to listen to her. What does she desire? A good gift for a woman is always a diamond. Actually, I am making a joke. Yes, it's nice to see jewellery on a woman, but I don't like jewellery, what it represents. The thought that that money would save the lives of hundreds of thousands of children. Can you compare that to a life?[23]

This is often my own reaction when I am presented with the possibility of paying a large sum of money for something that I don't really need: a meal in a restaurant, perhaps, or a shirt, or another pair of shoes. I have seen, first-hand, what real poverty looks like: the poverty of millions in Africa and in other parts of the world who have almost nothing to live on. The phrase 'a large sum of money' means very different things to different people, depending on who you are, where you live and what your circumstances are.

I recently did some research on pensions in South Africa. To address income poverty among the elderly, the South African government introduced in 2010 a means-tested state pension for all those over 60 years of age who have little or no other source of financial income. Currently the maximum amount payable is R1,520 per month, which is equivalent to around £90 per month. This old-age grant, as it is called, is now paid out each month to some three million South Africans, and for many of them this is all that they have to live on. Their situation, however, is much better than many other South Africans, because in 2015 one in three South Africans lived on less than R797 (around £48) per month.[24] This is what poverty looks like. This is what I keep in mind when I am tempted to spend money on something that is for me an extravagance or a luxury. I need to remember that Jesus says to me, 'When I was hungry, did you feed me? When I was naked, did you clothe me? When I was a stranger, did you welcome me?' (see Matthew 25:35–36).

At Easter 2017, after four years in office, Pope Francis spoke about what he saw as the most important challenge of that year:

> The first challenge I see before us concerns each and every one of us. It is the challenge to win over the globalisation of indifference. The destructive illness that turns our hearts to stone and makes us self-absorbed and only able to care for ourselves and our interests; it is the illness that renders us incapable of weeping, of feeling compassion, of letting us be hurt by others' suffering.[25]

To be a Christian in the age of consumerism is to be faced with a stark choice. Will we be conformed to the culture that surrounds us, or will we choose to live in a radical Christlike pattern of life? For all those who serve in Christian leadership and ministry, the call of God to holy living is inseparable from our public role. Yet we are daily faced with a complex set of choices and questions. We choose each day who and how we will serve: God or Mammon, to acquire or to simplify, to keep or to give away. The key to living faithfully as followers and servants of Jesus lies in knowing and guarding our own hearts, and always remembering who it is that we are serving: the one true living God.

6

The remedy: contentment

I have learned, in whatever state I am, to be content
PHILIPPIANS 4:11 (RSV)

One of the temptations that I often face when I have time to myself and I am away from public view is the temptation to acquire. Even though I have no need to buy more stuff, it's great to go shopping, especially when browsing and buying online is now so easy and convenient. Before I know it, I have acquired two more CDs and maybe some new clothing, and I have looked at some watches and maybe even a few cars. I'm not spending money that I don't have, so for me this is not about debt. For many others in our society, debt is a massive issue.

But for me, there is something vaguely troubling about this. There is a quick fix in acquiring stuff, a burst of adrenalin, an odd sense of having gained or achieved something. On reflection, though, I realise that often I have bought something that I don't need, and perhaps don't even want. Why is it that sometimes I come home with an object or an item that I have bought and then feel I don't really want after all? Sooner or later most of this stuff is going to end up in one of the local charity shops or the recycling centre. When this is the way we live now, it is difficult to see how we can ever claim to have contented hearts.

I can see that the remedy to this compulsive behaviour lies in a heart that is secure and content in knowing the unfailing love of God in Christ Jesus. If I am at peace with being the person that God has made me, and I know his complete care and provision for me, I don't need to be acquiring stuff to fill some vacuum in my life. But part of who I am is the false self that is crying out for attention and is always concerned to bolster my sense of self-identity and self-importance. I buy things that I don't need because they promise to fill a hole somewhere in my restless heart. This is not about needing more stuff. This is about me, about who I am, and the visible and tangible things with which I want to surround myself.

A good question to ask ourselves is this: is there ever a time when we are so satisfied with our surroundings that we do not need or want anything more? This may seem like some ideal state of detachment that we might experience during a holiday or a retreat in a beautiful, isolated place, perhaps in the mountains or on a remote island. But in our daily lives is it no longer possible to be content with what we have? My experience tells me that for most of us this is very difficult.

If we are to be content while surrounded by the hidden persuaders of consumerism and acquisition, we will need to be deeply secure in who we are and in our place in the universe. This is what Jesus promises us if we become his disciples and put our trust in him. Jesus spells this out in the sermon on the mount:

> Do not worry about your life, what you will eat or what you will drink, or about your body, what you will wear. Is not life more than food, and the body more than clothing? Look at the birds of the air; they neither sow nor reap nor gather into barns, and yet your heavenly Father feeds them.
> MATTHEW 6:25–26

For Jesus, life is about much more than food and drink and clothes. These are not the things that are truly and eternally important. They are here today and gone tomorrow. We are foolish if we set our hearts on such relatively insignificant things, when there are much greater riches to be found in knowing and serving the living God, and in enjoying his priceless gifts which are freely given to all his creatures.

Jesus teaches us that if we put our trust in God, our heavenly Father, and choose to live as his daughters and sons, we do not need to be anxious about any of our material needs. It is still right and prudent to work hard to earn a living and to provide for ourselves and our families. It is probably wise to have some savings and insurance policies to protect our most important possessions. But our hope, our trust and our security do not rest in these. If they do, we are indeed weak and vulnerable, because there is nothing on this earth that cannot be taken away by misfortune, disaster or illness.

Our deepest security is in God alone, and in his unfailing love and faithfulness. Those who choose to become disciples of Jesus Christ commit themselves to serving and working for the kingdom of God, above and before all earthly commitments and allegiances. As we make this choice, we are given God's promise that he will be our provider and our security, here on earth and for eternity. Jesus says, 'Strive first for the kingdom of God and his righteousness, and all these things will be given to you as well. So do not worry about tomorrow, for tomorrow will bring worries of its own. Today's trouble is enough for today' (Matthew 6:33–34). Or, as the Authorised Version (King James Bible) says, 'Sufficient unto the day is the evil thereof.'

Jesus does not tell us that we should not provide for the future, but rather that we should not be anxious. The key is to seek first the things of the kingdom of God and the righteousness and justice of God. This is what we live for. This is what life is all about. Then we can be secure in God's provision and care for us, for he is good and 'his steadfast love endures for ever' (Psalm 136). The provision and security that we find in God is far better and far greater than any bank account, insurance policy or beautiful home and property.

Our anxiety may be not only about financial or material provision. There is also 'status anxiety', to use the words of Alain de Botton, the author and philosopher. This is the widespread and pernicious anxiety about what others think of us. In his book *Status Anxiety*, de Botton defines this form of anxiety as:

a worry, so pernicious as to be capable of ruining extended stretches of our lives, that we are in danger of failing to conform to the ideals of success laid down by our society and that we may as a result be stripped of dignity and respect; a worry that we are currently occupying too modest a rung or are about to fall to a lower one. The anxiety is provoked by, among other elements, recession, redundancy, promotions, retirement, conversations with colleagues in the same industry, newspaper profiles of the prominent and the greater success of friends. Like confessing to envy (to which the emotion is related), it can be socially imprudent to reveal the extent of any anxiety and, therefore, evidence of the inner drama is uncommon, limited usually to a preoccupied gaze, a brittle smile or an over-extended pause after news of another's achievement.[26]

In our society, advertising often encourages us to acquire things that we hope will show others that we are successful and important people. An expensive sports car, a yacht or a beautiful home and garden are messages to anyone who wants to know: the owner of this is a person of substance.

But for followers of Jesus, this is problematic and troubling. Christians, just like anyone else, want and need the respect of others. We care about our dignity and we want others to take us seriously. However, we do not want to be seen as envious or avaricious, so we have to play these games in subtle ways. We can easily find ourselves comparing our achievements and even our possessions: the clothes we wear, the cars we drive, perhaps even the books and newspapers we read. But most of the time we don't say too much or tell those around us what we are really thinking.

The more secure we are in knowing that we are accepted and loved by God, the less we will find ourselves comparing and trying to prove our worth to others. We should not judge ourselves too harshly here. God knows our human frailty and our need for esteem. The needs of the false self are directly tied to the desire for esteem and significance. As I find my true self and become more and more the person that God has made me, I slowly but surely lose the need to compare myself with others. Status anxiety has less and less power over my heart. It becomes irrelevant to me whether I drive an old or a new car, or whether or not I am wearing the latest fashions.

Contentment is an attitude of the heart. It is a place of being at peace, with myself and with the world. Contentment flows from knowing that everything I have, and everything I am, comes from God. Every-thing is gift. We are simply stewards not owners. 'Yours, O Lord, are the greatness, the power, the glory, the victory, and the majesty; for all that is in the heavens and on the earth is yours,' said David before the assembly of the people of God. 'All things come from you, and of your own have we given you' (1 Chronicles 29:11, 14).

When we recognise this, we will find that contentment quickly turns to gratitude. It is easy to be thankful when we receive a generous gift, especially if we have no sense that this is something we are entitled to. A person whose heart is full of gratitude is a blessing to others and a joy to be around.

All that we have is given to us by God. It is ours to use, for his glory and for a season only. We glorify God when we use and enjoy and look after creation as he has commanded and intended. Objects can become friends, and they can be treasured: pieces of furniture or books handed down from parents or grandparents, precious gifts and garments that have seen us through many seasons. In our homes it is good to be surrounded by objects that have become friends over the years: a desk, a pen, a cricket bat, a picture on the wall. These are all good gifts, given by God, and blessings in good times and in adversity.

Contentment leads us to look with new eyes at all that we have and to ask ourselves, 'Do I need this?' We begin to clear the clutter in our lives and our homes. We find ourselves wanting to de-accumulate, to give away some of what we have so that others may benefit from what we have been holding on to. We find ourselves increasingly wanting to share our bread with the hungry, and to care for the homeless and the poor (see Isaiah 58:7).

But when our hearts are set on acquiring, everything becomes a commodity. Everything has a value to be measured and counted, gained and lost. In our culture, even time has become a commodity. Time is bought and lost. Time is money; it can be saved and spent, invested or wasted. In Africa there is a saying, 'You have the watches. We have the time.' They might equally say, 'You have the cars, the offices, the aeroplanes. We have the sky, the hills, the wind, the rain and the flowers.'

We may think that we own things, but we don't really. We cling to stuff. We use things and then discard many of them. But the earth is the Lord's, and all things are in his hands, whether we like it or not. If we know this, if we believe this and choose to live accordingly, we will find contentment and peace and joy. If we continue to pretend that the world is ours to divide up, exploit and devour, we are likely to be those whose restless hearts are never satisfied and always anxious.

When Jesus was tempted to turn stones into bread to satisfy his hunger, he said to the tempter, 'One does not live by bread alone, but by every word that comes from the mouth of God' (Matthew 4:4). Jesus also said in the beatitudes, 'Blessed are those who hunger and thirst for righteousness, for they will be filled' (Matthew 5:6). It is the things of God, his word and his righteousness, that truly satisfy our hunger. To be content is to be satisfied and to be at peace with who I am and with what I have. Blessed are those who know these great truths and who choose to live by them in a world of conspicuous consumption.

7

Achieve

How would you like to spend a day doing nothing? I'm not talking about doing absolutely nothing or simply lying in bed all day; I would find that very difficult, unless I was sufficiently ill or exhausted. When I was a child, my mother often used to sing a song called 'Busy Doing Nothing'. Those words have always intrigued me. To be busy doing nothing seems to imply simply enjoying life and not worrying about getting anything done or achieving anything. A child growing up on a farm could easily spend whole days busy doing nothing. I was once that child.

But now being busy doing nothing is a lost world. I am an adult. I have things to do. Adult life seems to have become an endless series of tasks to be accomplished and goals to be achieved. I watch the fishermen at the local fishing lake, and I wonder if I could spend the day simply sitting by the water, waiting for the fish to bite. Somehow I don't think that I could do this. When I was young, I used to wander up to the dam on our farm with my fishing rod and a can of worms, and spend a few happy hours by the water. Perhaps I even caught a few bluegills, because they were the only fish that were in the dam. They are too bony to eat, so I always threw them back. I was just having a good time. There was no result, nothing to take home. That didn't bother me at all. Gone fishing…

In 2002, I was asked to preach at a church in London on the subject 'Being countercultural Christians: freedom from achievementism'. I was surprised to be given this particular subject, but clearly even then this was an issue with which I was wrestling. London is a city where being a high achiever is very important to many people. But what is 'achievementism'? In my sermon, I defined achievementism as the preoccupation with success and achievement that is now so much part of our society. There is nothing wrong with achievements. It is good and indeed important to be able to look back at one's accomplishments, and to feel a sense of satisfaction at a job well done. The problem arises when we are constantly preoccupied and driven by the need to be achieving, to the point where this begins to rule our lives.

In my sermon, I talked about the realisation that when I try to stop and just do nothing, I find that this is not easy for me. I always have to be achieving something with my time, because otherwise I feel I am 'wasting time'. It is as though time is a scarce resource, and every minute has to be somehow accounted for before the great accountant in the sky. There is an old Irish saying, 'When God made time, he made plenty of it.' I have no doubt that God intends for us to use well the gifts that he has given us, including time. For me this means an intention to make good use of my days to enjoy and love God, to enjoy and love his creation, and to enjoy and love his people. This will mean that I am also being good to myself and finding an increase in peace, joy and love within my own heart. This surely is how God by his Holy Spirit is at work in me. But in our driven society and culture, this is not straightforward.

Much of the pressure behind achievementism in our society comes from the culture that we inhabit. This is a world of constant change, rush, noise and busyness. We seem to be always trying to do more, and to fit more work and more tasks into each day. In a world of ever-increasing acceleration, we can attempt to do three times as much in one day as our grandparents might have thought possible. We can attend meetings in different cities and even video-link across continents. We can respond to hundreds of emails and access vast quantities of information. And yet I often have to ask myself: what am I really achieving with a lot of what I do? I can look back at a great deal of time spent rushing around, travelling here, there and everywhere. I have been very busy, but when I reflect upon the life and teaching of Jesus, and on those things that contribute to the kingdom of God, I suspect that a lot of my time could have been better spent.

Malcolm Muggeridge wrote, 'There is nothing serious under the sun except love; of fellow mortals and of God.'[27] This, I think, tells the truth about life. So also does Ecclesiastes:

> For everything there is a season, and a time for every matter
>   under heaven:
>   a time to be born, and a time to die;
>   a time to plant, and a time to pluck up what is planted...
>   a time to weep, and a time to laugh;
>   a time to mourn, and a time to dance;
>   a time to throw away stones, and a time to gather stones
>   together;
>   a time to embrace, and a time to refrain from embracing.
> ECCLESIASTES 3:1–2, 4–5

This is how God has ordered his world. There is a time for everything. There is a time for work, and a time for rest (see Genesis 2:3; Exodus 20:8-11). We need to find the proper rhythm of life if we are to live in harmony with God and with one another.

Since 2002, when I preached in London on achievementism and countercultural Christianity, I have become ever more aware of how difficult it can be to break free of the compulsion to achieve, to always be doing something that seems to be important or valuable. Returning to a life of play, of simply enjoying ourselves without any goals or achievements, is difficult if not impossible for many of us. We are too wedded to winning, to proving ourselves and to getting things done.

Measuring and counting are habits that we can adopt to maintain a sense that we are doing something important. My false self constantly needs reassurance that what I am doing is somehow significant and that I am in control. Of course, this often is an illusion.

But numbers are a great way to feed the illusion. Counting is about achieving, measuring and comparing. It starts as a game, and becomes a way of life.

I am a keen birdwatcher, and I keep a list each year of the bird species that I have seen during that year. This motivates me to travel to different nature reserves, lakes and islands to see birds that I won't easily find anywhere else. But the downside for list-obsessed twitchers is that we can become primarily interested in the numbers on our personal lists. We may be sitting in a bird hide looking across a vast wetland with a spectacular sky and all the colours and sounds of birds wheeling and landing and diving, but if we are not seeing any new species, we are disappointed. Is it the list that counts, or is it simply being in the hide and taking in the beauty that surrounds me?

In 1983 Paul Simon released an album entitled *Hearts and Bones*. In a number of the songs, Simon wrestles with his own heartache and the pressure of our culture to be cerebral and acquisitive. A key song, which appears twice on the album, is called 'Think Too Much'. Simon sings about the way the analytical and rational left brain dominates the more creative and emotional right brain. Two other songs on the album, 'When Numbers Get Serious' and 'Cars Are Cars', resonate with my own life experience. I have to keep telling myself that cars are cars wherever you are. They are a means of transport. When I'm thinking about cars, I am usually thinking numbers: 325; A4; 2008; 38 mpg; £5,000; 0 to 60. When numbers get serious, our left brain is happy but the right brain is left behind and struggles to get a word in.

We need both sides of the brain, but our society is increasingly a left-brain society. The left brain helps us to control, manipulate and use the world pragmatically, while the 'right hemisphere sees the world from a metaphorical non-verbal, integrated and contextual way, open to experiences'.[28] Our openness to God, and to the leading of his Holy Spirit, is directly linked to our willingness to let go of the need to be in control, and to be open to the mystery of his loving purposes. We live by faith, not by being in control. Lists and numbers have their place, but they can too easily 'get serious' and start to rule our lives.

The preoccupation with measuring and control has become a dominant feature of modern organisational management. Many companies and organisations use key performance indicators (KPIs) and other similar tools to measure every aspect of their employees' work. Even the church is being drawn into this model of measuring productivity and value for money. 'How can we put money into something if we cannot measure what the outcomes or results will be?', I was asked by a church leader when I raised my own questions about some of this. But much local ministry does not respond easily or well to these models of management theory. Many employees are now expected to use smartphones and digital systems to continually transmit data and evaluate performance as they go about their daily work. It is difficult to see how a day spent in pastoral ministry, prayer and sermon preparation would be evaluated in this highly controlled system. How do I log and measure the value of time spent in visiting elderly parishioners or pondering what God is saying to the church through next Sunday's lectionary readings?

Many years ago, when I was at university studying business administration, I was taught a course on time-and-motion study. This is a business-efficiency technique first developed by Frederick Taylor in the USA in the early 20th century. Taylor worked as a shop foreman in a steel-making factory in Philadelphia and wanted to address inefficiencies and poor productivity, which he attributed to shirking and poorly motivated workers. He broke down each task into its component parts and devised highly efficient means of analysing and controlling every aspect of the production process. This led to the introduction of time cards, which recorded every minute spent working and on tea and lunch breaks. There was much resistance from unions, but gradually Taylor's ideas became integral to management theory and practice. We live today with the effect of this in virtually every workplace and organisation.

As Brett Frischmann and Evan Selinger write:

> The modern, digital version of Taylorism is more powerful than he could have ever imagined, and more dehumanising than his early critics could have predicted. Technological innovations have made it increasingly easy for managers to quickly and cheaply collect, process, evaluate and act upon massive amounts of information. In our age of big data, Taylorism has spread far beyond the factory floor... The first line of defence against Taylorism is to resist its relentless creep within and outside the workplace. Taylor's logic has become embedded in our everyday lives through our always-on digital environment. There is no easy solution to this.[29]

The danger for the church and for individual Christians is that we are conformed inwardly and outwardly to the prevailing culture of micromanagement and control. Taylorism becomes embedded in our own souls. We measure what we are doing, we evaluate and we demand more of ourselves and those around us. The church neglects or even forsakes the values of the kingdom of God – love, joy, peace, patience, gentleness, kindness, justice and truthfulness. We collude instead with a driven secular culture that constantly compares, competes and seeks to maximise profit and efficiency. When we go too far in accepting the practices and values of secular management culture, we weaken our own ability to hold before the world a different way of seeing and knowing what is important. Surely human beings are more important than profits and outcomes. We are not robots. We are made for greater things than this.

The consequences of a culture that is obsessed with achievement and productivity are everywhere to be seen. We are increasingly losing the ability to rest, to let go, to trust one another and to trust God. When we are always competing, we inhabit a world of winners and losers. Our anxiety is fuelled by our need each day to make sure that we remain on the winning side. In many modern professional sports, it is no longer the taking part that matters. We are told by our swimmers, athletes and cyclists that they are 'in it to win it'. If there always has to be a winner, there also has to be a loser. Even the word 'loser' has a vicious, painful tang to it.

If we are driven by achievementism, we are always competing and comparing. How am I doing? What am I hoping that others will notice? We damage our relationships with our colleagues and friends, and we poison our own hearts with the relentless and often unrealistic demands that we place on ourselves. I know, because I have tasted this bitter fruit. When this is how we live, we can never truly rest. There is always something more to be done, so we never fully let ourselves off the hook.

Some years ago I was working in the Diocese of Western Massachusetts. I heard a sermon one Sunday that has lodged in my heart. The preacher posed the question, 'Christianity: what's in it for me?' He paused for a while, and then said the answer is 'Nothing'. Following Jesus is not about me. It is all about Jesus. He is the Lord, and either he is Lord of all or he is not Lord at all.

I have thought long and hard about this. There are many blessings and many benefits that have come to me because I have become a follower of Jesus. But ultimately, I suspect the preacher was right. When we come back to the heart of worship, we find it's all about Jesus. It's not about me. It's not about my achievements, my glory or my success. It is about God, and about knowing and following Jesus Christ as Lord. If we are in any position of Christian leadership, we will need to guard our hearts carefully if we are not to be seduced by the temptations all around us to promote ourselves instead of him.

The contemplative response is the response of Jesus to his disciples when they asked him about who was the greatest. Jesus said, 'Whoever wishes to become great among you must be your servant, and whoever wishes to be first among you must be slave of all. For the Son of Man came not be served but to serve, and to give his life a ransom for many' (Mark 10:43–45).

8

The remedy: detachment

Indeed I count everything as loss because of the surpassing worth of knowing Christ Jesus my Lord.

PHILIPPIANS 3:8 (RSV)

Detachment is an act of spiritual freedom. It is the virtue of habitually choosing out of freedom not compulsion, fear or routine. Therefore, it is a virtue that allows a person to review competing goods and choose that which most fulfils one's life ideals or values.

Howard Gray[30]

Detachment is freedom. It is a contemplative response to competing demands and attractions, because it is rooted in a heart that is settled and held firm in its ultimate allegiance. Detachment flows from choosing this day who I will serve, and then allowing the implications of this choice to mould every part of my life and my behaviour.

Achievement is gaining credit or esteem. Detachment is counting all things as loss because of the surpassing worth of knowing Christ Jesus our Lord.

In Galatians 5:1, Paul pleads with the Christians in Galatia: 'For freedom Christ has set us free. Stand firm, therefore, and do not submit again to a yoke of slavery.' If our hearts are being continually pulled and pushed in differing directions through achievementism, compulsive behaviour and self-indulgent habits, we are not free. For those who have chosen to follow Jesus as Lord, the way to freedom comes from placing Jesus at the centre of the whole of life. We then need daily discernment to reveal to us what place in our lives we will give to each of the demands and the attractions that surround us.

The key is knowing where our ultimate allegiance lies; lip service is not enough. The danger for us is to name Jesus as our Lord, but to live our lives in the service of other clamouring lords and masters. Jesus said, 'Not everyone who says to me, "Lord, Lord", will enter the kingdom of heaven, but only one who does the will of my Father in heaven' (Matthew 7:21).

This is a significant challenge for Christians living in a consumerist and individualist society. We can all too easily be seen as those who call ourselves Christians but live our lives according to the same values as everyone else around us. The only discernible difference may be that we have a few religious habits, such as going to church and saying our prayers. To be holy means to be set apart, to be different, to be salt and light to the world around us. If our lives and our behaviour do not reflect the character and actions of Jesus, we become hypocrites, actors, pretending to be something that we are not. The credibility of the Christian faith depends on the example and actions of those who claim to be Christian. Are we making up patterns of work, of lifestyle and even of worship, and calling them Christian, when they are primarily all about our own status, comfort and security?

Detachment is the remedy for much of this acquiescence and accommodation to the world's values. Detachment is not apathy or indifference. We believe passionately in the one who is the source of all life, the almighty God, and in his Son, Jesus Christ our Lord. We therefore choose to live only for him, and to his glory. All our other choices and preferences flow from this. Our behaviour, our values and our example flow directly from the values and example of Jesus. This may set us at odds with those around us who are more willing to accept the expectations and demands of a driven, goal-oriented society.

As we learn detachment, we are enabled to enjoy God's good gifts without being seduced by any of them. I can enjoy birdwatching, running marathons and driving my car, but I am not controlled by any of these. I do not have to be constantly ticking boxes or achieving goals. I can take them up, and I can let them go. There are so many good things that are given to us by God: a good meal; a glass of wine; a cup of coffee; holidays and travel; clothing and shoes; art and music; smartphones and computer games. They all can have their place in our lives, but they all carry the shadow of their potential to become idols, addictions and obsessions.

Many of those in Christian leadership and ministry will know that our work can become our god. David Watson, towards the end of his life, came to the realisation that the Lord's work should never have become more important to him than his love for and intimacy with the Lord. Watson wrote in his book *Fear No Evil*, 'He showed me that all my preaching, writing and other ministry was absolutely *nothing* compared to my love relationship with him.'[31]

Through detachment we learn that it does not matter whether we win or lose, whether we are first of all or last of all. We are enabled to resist the inner compulsions and the outer expectations that otherwise would drive us on and keep us from a depth of intimacy with God.

As we grow in the practice of contemplation, learning to live from a heart that is centred on God, we will find ourselves increasingly attuned to our need for detachment. We will recognise the small compulsions and addictions that many, if not all, of us carry around. Some of these may become major problems of addictive behaviour, and may be difficult to break. Others are small but sometimes subtle habits that we fall into, and need to arrest. Fasting is the discipline, the corrective, that helps us to surrender all things to God, and to seek him for who he is. When we fast, we deny ourselves food or other aspects of normal daily living, in order to say to our bodies, appetites and compulsions, 'You do not rule me.' I remember some years ago an elderly priest who smoked a pipe saying to me, 'When Lent comes around I put away my pipe and tobacco, and I do without them until Lent is over. I am just saying to them, "You are not my Lord and you need to know your place."'

From time to time it is good also to fast from working and from activity. This is partly about our God-given need for rest, but this is more than simply rest and sleep. We stop; we wait; we listen; we become still; we do nothing for a while. This is a vital spiritual discipline in our driven and demanding world of work, especially for all those in Christian leadership. It is not easy to lay down our to-do lists and our need for action. When I try to do this, I find that my mind quickly latches on to something that I could be doing, or planning, or achieving. There is a discipline that is required in letting go of all this and learning simply to be.

St John of the Cross, the great Spanish mystic and poet, is perhaps best known for his poem 'Dark Night of the Soul'. He also has much to say about detachment as an essential part of the contemplative life. He is uncompromising in his assertion that complete detachment from created things is necessary in order for us to experience a deep and intimate encounter with God. According to William H. Shannon:

> John of the Cross denies neither the goodness of creatures nor the need to use them. He probes deeper to the very roots of the problem posed by creatures. *The problem is not in creatures but in ourselves.* It is not the creatures but the *desire* for them that impedes our quest for God. John affirms without reservation 'that desire of creatures as ends in themselves cannot coexist with the desire of God as our true end'.[32]

St John of the Cross describes the call to detachment in these very challenging words:

> In order to have pleasure in everything
> Desire to have pleasure in nothing.

In order to arrive at possessing everything
Desire to possess nothing.
In order to arrive at being everything
Desire to be nothing.
In order to arrive at knowing everything
Desire to know nothing.[33]

This description of detachment may seem too severe and perhaps even offensive or scandalous to 21st-century Christians. But read carefully what John is saying here. The issue is not pleasure, possessions, position or knowledge. This is all about desire. These words are like a magnifying glass used to concentrate light on to one fixed point to ignite a fire. What is our deepest desire? Do we desire God so much that all other desires are as nothing to us? Are we willing to forsake all and follow Jesus? At the heart of Christian faith is this fundamental choice. Who do we serve: God or Mammon? Who do we love: God or our own self-interest? Who or what do we desire: God or pleasure, possessions and position? With God, it has to be all or nothing. Shannon says, 'It is not pleasure, knowledge, possession or being as such that must be "darkened" or "mortified", but only the passion of desire for these things.'[34]

In John's gospel, the risen Jesus appears to a small group of his disciples early one morning beside the Sea of Galilee. After they have finished breakfast, Jesus asks Simon Peter three times, 'Simon, do you love me?' We are told that Simon Peter was hurt that Jesus should ask him three times, 'Do you love me?' But the question is very important. To each of those who call ourselves his disciples, Jesus says, 'Do you truly love me? Do you love me more than all of those other calls on your heart?'

If we are not to lose our first love, we need to guard our hearts. We learn to practise detachment, letting go of all other loves, desires and demands. Life will give us many opportunities for this. When our patience is tested, when we have to wait for something that we want or need, we can quietly in our hearts let go of our desire to have our own way and place ourselves unreservedly in God's care. We trust in his provision, whatever that may be. We do not need to be constantly achieving something or always appearing to be busy. We do not need to be in control or to be given recognition. We empty ourselves of all this and take on the nature of a servant for Jesus' sake. Our trust is in God and in his unfailing love for us. He alone is our first love, and we find our rest in him.

There will be times in all our lives when we experience a kind of pruning, a removing or curtailing of aspects of our lives that are important or precious to us. Pruning involves cutting back, trimming away excess foliage and removing dead wood. In gardening, pruning is essential to ensure healthy growth and good fruit. Jesus says, 'I am the true vine, and my Father is the vine-grower… Every branch that bears fruit he prunes to make it bear more fruit' (John 15:1–2). The book of Hebrews speaks of the discipline of the Father in the lives of his children: 'Now, discipline always seems painful rather than pleasant at the time, but later it yields the peaceful fruit of righteousness to those who have been trained by it' (Hebrews 12:11).

Pruning and discipline are necessary for us if we are to learn detachment. Sometimes through weakness and loss, through sickness and pain, we find ourselves thrown on to a new dependence on God. We may be forced to let go of cherished plans and dreams. At the time this may feel harsh, and certainly can be unpleasant and uncongenial. Through pruning and discipline, and sometimes through suffering, our hearts may be purified, as we seek the Lord in new ways and offer ourselves more fully to him. In detachment we know that God is love, and his love is all we need. His love is sufficient for us. Nothing else ultimately can satisfy us or keep us secure.

In detachment we find our vocation, our true calling from God. Other calls and other desires are relinquished. We let go of all that is not God's call, God's love, God's rich beauty. We are set free in Christ to know God and to serve him with our whole heart, soul, mind and strength. We choose who we will serve, and we work out each day the meaning and implications of that choice. In this, we know a quality of life, peace and joy that achievementism and compulsive activity can never give us.

9

Indulge

When I was studying theology in Oxford, a new American-style doughnut shop opened in the town. The doughnuts were freshly baked, and I was young and athletic, regularly running, canoeing and playing rugby. I had a healthy appetite and soon found that I could eat my way through a whole box of four freshly baked doughnuts, straight out of the oven. There was only one problem: when I had finished the box, I felt a faint sense of guilt. Something about the level of indulgence made me feel uneasy, as though for some reason it can't be right to sit on my own and eat four doughnuts one after the other. Besides that, I knew that if I tried to eat one more I would probably be sick.

In a more puritanical age than our own, there was a lot of guilt attached to indulging ourselves. Gluttony was a sin, and probably still is. But we are less sure about all of this now, because the world of advertising and marketing is sending us a constant message that it's good to indulge yourself – spend more; eat more; drink more; gamble more. The hidden persuaders are all around us. In fact, many of them are in plain sight, constantly telling us to go ahead and eat, drink and be merry. Guilt is pushed to the margins. Our economy depends on consumers spending more and more and therefore consuming more and more. We are told that this is necessary in order to sustain economic growth and to provide an ever-increasing standard of living.

I am writing this in December, a few weeks before Christmas. We are now in Advent, and even Advent calendars have become heavily commercialised. The message seems to be that Advent is a wonderful time to indulge yourself each day, as you open your

Advent calendar. One product from a well-known upmarket cosmetic company offers 'a skincare or make-up surprise for you each day: 24 beauty gifts to count the days until Christmas and bring you joy before the big holiday!' Or you could go for 'a deliciously filled wooden Advent calendar with small numbered doors, each one filled with an exciting selection of sweets and chocolates'. None of this is cheap, and then there is Christmas itself. Our local supermarket is telling us that 'while we indulge in mince pies, turkey and Brussels sprouts, there's a world of Christmas offerings to explore' from other parts of the world, from Germany to Guyana. Christmas is a very special and important time for me, as it is for so many people, but I do feel that the meaning of Christmas is being strangled by sheer overindulgence and excess.

To indulge yourself is to yield to an inclination or a desire to enjoy yourself and to satisfy an appetite. When we are hungry, we enjoy a good meal. When we are thirsty on a long hot summer's day, a cold refreshing drink is just what we need. We can enjoy the gifts that God has given us, at the right time and in the right place, and many of the best gifts are free: the beauty of a sunrise; a friendly greeting; a walk through the fields; a good night's sleep. All of these are gifts we can receive with gratitude and joy.

The problem arises for us when our appetites control us. We seem to be surrounded by too much of everything, and we need to be able to say no to some of this. In fact, we need to be able to say no to all of this at some point, because otherwise these things have begun to rule us. The false self feeds on the desires and attachments that keep alive the illusion that my life is all about me. I want to be fed, entertained and satisfied. I need pleasure and comfort to keep this 'me-first' self occupied and happy, knowing that it is 'me' who matters in my life. Then I start to think that God is there in order to look after me, and to provide me with the good things that I need and want.

Selfishness is the state of being controlled by the desires and attachments that feed the false self. Detachment allows us to place

God in his rightful place in our lives and hearts, and to find freedom from being ruled and controlled by any other desire or allegiance. As followers of Jesus, we seek to leave behind the slavery of being ruled by our own desires. If we are addicted to being consumers, to buying and eating and owning and indulging, we cannot meet with God in the centre of our lives.

In 21st-century western society, indulgence is the air we breathe. It seems that we are bringing up our children to think and believe that our main purpose in life is to be consumers. There are also many in our society for whom this rotten state of affairs is simply a daily reminder of how left behind they are. Those on a low, or no, income see the opulence and affluence that is paraded daily before us, and know that this is a world where every day the rich are getting richer and the poor are getting more and more left behind. They live with the despair, deprivation and anger that is the downside of a market- and profit-driven consumer society.

How do we indulge? Let me count the ways. We indulge in food. Look at the overstocked supermarket shelves, the expensive restaurants and the double- and triple-chocolate extravaganzas that are offered for our pleasure and indulgence. When I was a child, cake and chocolate were treats, not something I tasted very often. I now eat chocolate and cake every week, maybe even every day.

We indulge in drink. We have fizzy drinks, lattes and cappuccinos, beer and wine, whisky and gin. I spend a lot of time in cafes, and I am glad that there are so many around. When I was a student, every day I went out with friends to a bar somewhere to drink beer and talk and pass the time. When my student days were over, I stopped going to bars, but a friend of mine was not able to. I met him about five years after we left university, and after a few minutes' conversation I realised that he was an alcoholic. My life had moved on, but his never did.

We indulge in sex. We may not do so personally and physically, but we are surrounded by sex. Sex is everywhere: in advertising; on television and in movies; in magazines, books and newspapers; and of course on the internet. A few years ago, I was sitting in a coffee shop looking at my new iPod touch, browsing the apps, when I suddenly found myself looking at a photograph of a completely naked young woman. I thought I had just been exploring this new world of social-networking sites that others in my office were excited about. What was going on here? I quickly discovered that this is the new reality, and that I need to be very careful in how I use the internet. I have no desire ever to watch pornography. I know that there are things that I do not want to look at and that I do not want to see. But I know that, like everyone else, I can be tempted in this area, and there is always the thin end of the wedge.

We indulge in technology – in smartphones, computer games and social networks. Many of these can be seriously addictive. We indulge in gadgets and machines, travel and experiences. We indulge in shopping. We buy things that we don't need, just for the pleasure of it. We indulge in comfort, pleasure and luxury, because it is constantly offered to us and because sometimes we can't resist. We are the consumers with open mouths, just waiting and wanting for more to fill that bottomless pit of desire.

Eating four doughnuts one after the other is a little excessive, but nothing serious. The slippery slope lies when this becomes a way of life, a daily habit of excess and indulgence. Often we are so caught up in this that we do not even recognise it for what it is. Those who call Jesus their Lord and Master will need to go back to the gospels and weigh this way of life against the life and teaching of Jesus.

Jesus said, 'Blessed are the pure in heart, for they will see God' (Matthew 5:8). To be pure in heart is to surrender ourselves to God and to his purposes for us. Søren Kierkegaard expresses this clearly in the profound title of his book *Purity of Heart Is To Will One Thing* (1938). The pure in heart are blessed because they have come to find and see God within their own hearts, in the deepest centre of their being. To be pure in heart is to become the person that God has made me and called me to be. It is to become my true self. As we shake loose the demands of self-indulgence and the desires of the false self, which have no lasting value or reality, we see the world in the light of the eternal realities of the all-present and all-knowing God of love. We are set free in Christ to see things as they really are.

Some measure of simplicity in our lives will be essential if we are to know this freedom. We have to look carefully at how we live. We pray for the discernment to see where our hearts are being held by the clutter and clamour that surround us. We then begin to take action to deal with the 'muchness' and the 'manyness' that crowd out the still small voice of the Spirit of God.

We know in our hearts that our freedom is rooted not in having more fun, more pleasure and more comfort, but in knowing God and his love for us in Christ. There will be times when we may need to discipline ourselves in order to restore a proper perspective and ordering of our lives. It may be necessary for us to withdraw for a while to the wilderness in some form, to discover again our need of God and our dependence on him. As we enter into retreat, fasting or solitude, we can, like Jesus in the desert, recognise the tempter for who he is and rebuke him in the power of God's word.

The wilderness in the Bible is the place of refining, of returning to the Lord and of hearing his voice anew. From Moses to John the Baptist, from Elijah to Jesus, the desert and the wilderness have been essential in hearing the call of God and in seeing things as they really are. The desert is a place of silence and solitude, where comfort and pleasure are stripped away. It is a place of thirst and hunger. This may be uncomfortable for us to hear, but if we are to become free in Christ, we will need to learn to deny many of our most ingrained and cherished desires and appetites. We then find ourselves learning what it is to depend totally on God.

I once spent a few days in silent retreat at a Benedictine abbey in England. It was mid-February, and the weather was cold. I had chosen to sleep in a beautiful medieval gatehouse. After a couple of hours, I started to think, 'What on earth am I doing here? I am *so* cold.' But then I remembered that Jesus chose to go to the wilderness for 40 days and nights, where he did not enjoy the comforts of home. Maybe it would be good for me also to do without central heating and home comforts for just a short while.

To be free in Christ means living for Christ alone, serving only him. This means that our goal throughout life will be that our hearts do not become, in the words of Thomas Merton, 'dominated or even influenced by any attachment to any created thing or to (our) own selves or to any gift of God'.[35] For many people in our society, our minds and hearts are so dominated by our own desires and attachments that we now have but a dim and dismal grasp of the life of God as taught and revealed in Jesus.

I am reminded of the call of John the Baptist to all those who would be the ministers, stewards and messengers of the Lord:

> The voice of one crying out in the wilderness:
> 'Prepare the way of the Lord,
>   make his paths straight.'
> MATTHEW 3:3

John the Baptist also said, 'Bear fruit worthy of repentance' (Matthew 3:8). The fruit of hearts that are pure will be lives that over-flow with the love and compassion of Jesus, and that proclaim the way of the Lord to a world of illusions and brokenness.

10

The remedy: self-control

The fruit of the Spirit is love, joy, peace, patience, kindness, generosity, faithfulness, gentleness, and self-control. There is no law against such things. And those who belong to Christ Jesus have crucified the flesh with its passions and desires. If we live by the Spirit, let us also be guided by the Spirit.
GALATIANS 5:22–25

When I was a student in South Africa in the early 1970s, one of the people who guided and nudged me towards the possibility of ordained Anglican ministry was Bishop Bill Burnett. At the time Bill was the bishop of Grahamstown in the Cape, and he took me for a long walk along the beach in the Eastern Cape. He listened carefully as I spoke about the extraordinary way in which I had seen God at work in my life and in the lives of many of my friends. A few months later, Bishop Bill replied to a letter that I had written to him about being a youth worker in his diocese. 'It seems to me,' he wrote, 'that you should now consider offering yourself for the priesthood of the Anglican Church.' He later became Archbishop of Cape Town and leader of the Anglican Church in South Africa. Bishop Bill was a traditional Anglican whose ministry was transformed following a remarkable experience of being filled by the power and presence of the Holy Spirit. He became a leader in the worldwide charismatic movement, which significantly impacted my own life during those years.

The Holy Spirit is the third person of the holy Trinity, and yet often in the history of the church the life-changing power of the Holy Spirit has been overlooked. The Holy Spirit was given by Jesus to his church so that it would be empowered to live as Jesus had taught us to live, and to be his witnesses to the world.

Bishop Bill was a leader who helped me to discover the power and the reality of the Holy Spirit at a critical point in my life. Among many other charismatic leaders who became well known during this period was J. Keith Miller. He was a writer and speaker from Austin, Texas, who had, like Bill Burnett, discovered the life-changing power of knowing Jesus Christ and living in the power and joy of the Holy Spirit. He wrote a book called *The Taste of New Wine* (1965), which I was given to read when I experienced the work of the Holy Spirit in my own life. This book has gone on to sell over two million copies worldwide.

Some 20 years ago, in the early 1990s, I was interested to pick up a new book by Miller, called *Hope in the Fast Lane*. This was a very different kind of book from *The Taste of New Wine*. The book is an honest description, written after years of apparently successful high-profile ministry, of how Miller had to face up to his own problems of addiction and compulsive behaviour. The book deals with the reality of life for many people in our stress-ridden, high-pace world. Miller painfully comes to recognise the problems that are being caused for himself and those around him by his addiction to work and busyness, his compulsions and his denial. Miller writes:

> When I became a Christian I had been told that God promised to give us his peace, which would transcend the problems of the world. It was strongly suggested that our hearts don't have to be troubled or afraid. And when in my late twenties I made a serious commitment to become one of God's people, I was overjoyed to discover that I did find a happiness and peace that I had not known before. For several years I was an enthusiastic witness to the fact that God can and really does bring us relief from our fears and anxieties.[36]

But slowly Miller's life began to unravel. He says:

My compulsive working no longer brought me the things I wanted. Instead, as the demands on me piled up, my attempts to 'manage' the people close to me accelerated. I became more controlling and had more 'suggestions' about how people should run their lives. I drank more wine before dinner, and during dinner, to 'calm my nerves'. From my perspective, my family and business associates didn't respond the way I hoped. And they made what seemed to me to be unreasonable demands on me. Some of the close ones pointed to my 'hidden' selfishness and made infuriating hints that I was not the hardworking, sensitive, and generous man I was trying to be. This made me very angry. I argued and justified myself and my actions at every turn with smooth explanations of my point of view.[37]

Miller found that, although he knew that he was not happy and that something was not right, he simply could not stop: 'I was bone-tired, but I couldn't seem to stop and rest from the all-encompassing busyness I had created with my compulsive behaviour.'[38]

Self-discipline and self-denial are the obvious solutions to overindulgence. But self-discipline is not easy, and simply trying to exercise greater self-control will not work for many people. The problem with self-indulgence, as with other forms of compulsive behaviour, is that although we may feel a sense of guilt and shame, we may also find ourselves unable to change. We are caught in a cycle of doing things that we do not really enjoy, being filled with regret and possibly penitence, perhaps making resolutions to do better in the future, and then going back to square one. We may say that we are depending on God's grace and the power of the Holy Spirit, but if we are living in denial, it is very difficult for grace to break through. The Holy Spirit works gently and graciously in our hearts. But sometimes our false self is able to resist the work of the Spirit and postpone the transformation of our hearts from 'me-first' to 'Jesus-first', which is the purpose of the Holy Spirit for us.

When we have developed a long-standing pattern of compulsive behaviour, whether over-eating, sex-addiction, alcohol abuse or gambling, it is often no help whatsoever to be told by some well-meaning friend that we need to be more disciplined. Self-control is one of the nine fruits of the Holy Spirit (Galatians 5:22–23), but in order to receive these fruits, and to live a life of love, peace and joy, a radical change in our own hearts is required. Sometimes this can only happen when we come to the end of our own resources, perhaps through some experience of brokenness and suffering. This may be painful at the time, but for some this is the only way that we can move towards becoming the person God has created us to be.

Miller describes, in *Hope in the Fast Lane*, how following a major health scare he came to recognise his compulsive behaviour as a form of addiction. He calls this the 'sin-disease'. Essentially what Miller is describing is the preoccupation with self, the 'me-first' way of living that can afflict Christians even while they are professing Jesus as Lord, working hard in his service, and perhaps leading churches and writing books.

Denial is a serious issue for anyone with patterns of compulsive behaviour. We lock up our inner selves with a hard outer shell to protect us and defend us from criticism and even from loving advice that threatens our established way of functioning. We develop strategies to ward off any honest discussion of what is happening. We say, 'Don't tell me what to do,' 'Don't waste my time,' 'I thought you were my friend,' and so on. Our false self thinks that it knows best what keeps us safe and strong, and will do anything to maintain this inner security. But being strong and in control will never bring us the peace for which our true self is longing. Our true peace and happiness come from letting go, and from recognising our dependence on God for all that we need.

Denial prevents us from becoming vulnerable and from being willing to listen to those who long to help us but just can't find a way to get through. Miller says:

Work addicts or overeaters may never realise that their compulsive behaviour is a message from God trying to warn them that there's something out of kilter at the centre of their lives – that they have transgressed the basic rule of human life by putting themselves and their God-playing at the centre where only God can make life work. The message gets louder and louder through increasingly serious emotional and then physical symptoms: emotional symptoms like anxiety, lack of sleep, depression, irrational outbursts, and resentment, and physical symptoms like headaches, arthritis, ulcers, colitis, certain heart conditions, strokes, in some cases a series of dangerous 'accidents', and – some physicians believe – even cancer.[39]

Miller's experience was that, in recognising his addiction for what it was, he was able to find significant help and insight through the principles contained in the twelve-step programme of Alcoholics Anonymous. Many variations of the twelve-step programme have emerged around the world in recent years, including Narcotics Anonymous, Cocaine Anonymous, Co-dependents Anonymous, Gamblers Anonymous and Sexual Compulsives Anonymous. There is even Workaholics Anonymous, which I suspect a number of clergy could find helpful. Miller writes, 'The ambience of love and spiritual integrity in these groups is unlike anything I have seen. They have taken the tools of authentic faith that some of us had rejected, and God has created an incredible community of his people.'[40]

The principles that underpin the twelve-step approach are that we admit that we are powerless over our addiction or compulsion, that we come to believe a power greater than ourselves can restore us to sanity, and that we make a decision to surrender our lives to God as we understand him. We will then need to take practical steps, including repentance for past behaviour, restitution wherever possible to those we have hurt, and a commitment to prayer and to deepening our relationship with God. Another core part of this new way of living is that we recognise we cannot do this on our own. We will need a community around us to whom we can be accountable, and on whom we depend for support and care because we know that we are weak and vulnerable.

The recognition of our own weakness is central to growing in holiness. As long as we are determined to 'do it my way', to be strong and in control, we cannot truly open ourselves to the grace and power of the Holy Spirit. Paul says, 'Whenever I am weak, then I am strong' (2 Corinthians 12:10). He speaks of his own problem, the 'thorn in the flesh', which plainly troubled him greatly, though we do not know what this painful thorn was. Paul writes, 'Three times I appealed to the Lord about this, that it would leave me, but he said to me, "My grace is sufficient for you, for power is made perfect in weakness"' (2 Corinthians 12:8–9).

The remedy for self-indulgence and for all our patterns of compulsive behaviour is the fruit of the Holy Spirit: love, joy, peace, patience, kindness, generosity, faithfulness, gentleness and self-control (Galatians 5:22–23). These qualities are the true reflection of the life and character of Jesus. We will only be able to show these to others as we are enabled, perhaps first of all, to show them to ourselves. If we are hard on ourselves, we are also likely to be hard on those around us. We become patient with ourselves, gentle and kind to ourselves, compassionate to ourselves. As our hearts are changed by the indwelling power of the Holy Spirit, we are filled with his love and joy and with the peace that passes understanding. We become faithful to others, because faithfulness has become our true nature. We may fail from time to time, but we are held by God's grace and love. We find self-control, because self-control is a gift from God to us when our hearts are held secure in his love and satisfied by his promises. We no longer need patterns of addictive behaviour. They lose their power, and our chains fall off, our hearts are free.

This is how self-control in the power of the Holy Spirit takes shape. We will find our hearts drawn to new patterns of daily life that are life-giving and life-affirming for us. We may be led to set these out for ourselves in some form of 'rule of life'. A Christ-centred rule of life is not a list of regulations or laws; it is rather a set of priorities that have been formed through prayer and a desire to live each day in ways that are pleasing to God and life-giving for ourselves and those around us.

My own rule of life has been formed over many years, and helps me to choose each day how to spend my time, money and energy. Sometimes I am able to live closely to this pattern, while at other times, perhaps if I am ill or very busy, I will have to be gentle with myself and recognise that I don't or can't do all that I would ideally like to do. I know that Jesus is faithful, and this enables me to be faithful. He speaks to me through my heart's desires and leads me in paths of righteousness. The more I live in the way that Christ has taught me, the more I want to avoid getting caught in the entanglements of the world that mess up my closest relationships and my own life.

The rule of life that I have found to be most helpful for me in nourishing my spirit and my sense of God's presence looks something like this:

- A daily practice of prayer, morning, noon and evening, and before I go to sleep. This includes reflection on my own life and my need for God's forgiveness, reading the Bible, contemplative prayer and intercession.
- Belonging and participating in the life of my local church community.
- Regularly receiving Holy Communion.
- Prioritising time for my family and for nurturing my closest relationships.
- Making time for friends.
- Serving God through faithful ministry and witness to Christ.
- Seeking ways to serve the poor and to show compassion for those who have less than I do.
- Giving generously to the work of Jesus in different ways. I start

with a tithe, a tenth of my income, and seek to be generous with all that I have.

- Choosing to live simply and to care for the world that God has made.
- To exercise regularly, eat and drink wisely, rest when I should rest, and avoid indulging my appetites in ways that are not honouring to God nor healthy for my own well-being.

As I practise this way of life, I can see that I am living in an ever-deepening relationship of love for God. I am able to be led by the Holy Spirit, day by day, and I am discovering his fruit growing and maturing in my own heart. This is the way of love, joy and peace, and this is the way of faithfulness and self-control. These are fruits that flow from a heart that is honestly seeking God each day. Self-control cannot be imposed. Self-control flows from a heart that desires to be holy, and that is open to God and to truthfulness before him. We know that we are weak, yet he is strong, and he is able to transform our inmost being and to make us his holy people.

Part Three

The contemplative heart

11

Contemplation: the way to communion with God

In his address to the Synod of Bishops in Rome in October 2012, then Archbishop of Canterbury Rowan Williams spoke about the profound connection between contemplation and the task of evangelisation, the making known of the good news of Jesus to the world. He said:

> Contemplation is very far from being just one kind of thing that Christians do: it is the key to prayer, liturgy, art and ethics, the key to the essence of a renewed humanity that is capable of seeing the world and other subjects in the world with freedom – freedom from self-oriented, acquisitive habits and the distorted understanding that comes from them. To put it boldly, contemplation is the only ultimate answer to the unreal and insane world that our financial systems and our advertising culture and our chaotic and unexamined emotions encourage us to inhabit. To learn contemplative practice is to learn what we need so as to live truthfully and honestly and lovingly. It is a deeply revolutionary matter.[41]

There is something important that seems to be almost hidden in these words of Williams. It is as though he is pointing us to a great and beautiful work of art that to our eyes is barely visible, hidden in the shadows. If contemplation is the key to the essence of a renewed humanity that is capable of seeing the world and other subjects in the world with the freedom that Jesus promises, we need to know what contemplation is. Yet many Christians have only a dim idea of what Williams is talking about here. I myself for many years had little understanding of what is meant by 'contemplative practice'. We are so enmeshed in the rational world that we chiefly comprehend even spiritual reality through the lens of our mind, and its capacity to analyse, process and decide. But contemplation asks us to make the leap from the mind to the heart in order that we may truly know God.

Theophan the Recluse was a Russian Orthodox monk who died in 1894. He wrote a number of books on the Christian life, prayer and spirituality. In his teaching on prayer, Theophan writes:

> I will remind you of only one thing: one must descend with the mind into the heart, and there stand before the face of the Lord, ever present, all seeing within you. The prayer takes a firm and steadfast hold, when a small fire begins to burn in the heart. Try not to quench this fire, and it will become established in such a way that the prayer repeats itself, and then you will have within you a small murmuring stream.[42]

Theophan is describing the way in which we can learn to practise the presence of God in all the tasks and activities of our daily lives. As the prayer of the heart becomes part of who we are, we find that we are increasingly able to 'pray without ceasing', as Paul says in 1 Thessalonians 5:17. This is not a matter of saying prayers constantly but of being continually held in the presence of God. Contemplation, and contemplative practice, is chiefly concerned with opening the heart to the love of God in Christ. Understanding with our minds is important, but in a relationship it is the giving of the heart in love that is essential.

'I give you my heart,' we say to the one we love. When we truly love someone, we hopefully will think carefully about what we are doing. We will act with understanding and thoughtfulness. But love, freely and fully given, is not a calculation or a judgement. Love is a response from deep within us to someone or something that we care about. Love is a giving of ourselves that flows from the heart, from our inmost being, and is known to be genuine only when it is revealed in actions of compassion and self-sacrifice. When we give our hearts, we give ourselves. We lay down our lives for one another.

To learn contemplative practice is to engage ourselves every day in an unconditional opening of our hearts, our deepest and truest selves, to the God whose name is Love. He is the God and Father of our Lord Jesus Christ, who so loved the world that he gave his only Son in order that all those who put their trust in him would not perish but have everlasting life (John 3:16). 'We love because he first loved us' (1 John 4:19), and so perhaps the deepest and truest form of prayer is contemplation, the offering of our own hearts and our deepest selves in love to God, who first loved us.

How do we do this? In the Christian tradition there are a number of methods of contemplative prayer, the prayer of the heart, that are widely used and recognised. In the eastern monastic tradition, the practice of simply calling upon the name of the Lord Jesus Christ is considered to be most important, as the sacramental power of the name of Jesus is believed to open the heart to the indwelling power of the Holy Spirit. The Jesus Prayer – 'Lord Jesus Christ, Son of God, have mercy on me, a sinner' – has in recent years spread into the lives and practice of many western Christians. The words of the prayer and the name of Jesus become one with the very beating of the heart, and fill the whole being with warmth and love.

Lectio divina (divine reading) is a form of contemplative prayer in which we read a short passage of the Bible, and then slowly and quietly allow God to meet us and to speak to us through his word. There are four steps in this process. We start with *lectio* (reading), and then after a time of quiet we move to *meditatio* (meditation), then more silence, then *oratorio* (prayer), and then finally *contemplatio* (contemplation). We read the passage carefully at the beginning of each stage, and we open our hearts to God in the silence that follows. *Lectio divina* is a way of using the Bible in prayer not primarily to increase our understanding, but rather to deepen our relationship with God through the experience of his love, as revealed in his word.

Christian meditation is a widely used method that 'involves the repetition of a single word faithfully and lovingly during the time of meditation'.[43] This again is an ancient Christian way of prayer that was recovered for modern Christians by the Benedictine monk John Main (1926–82). In this method, our emphasis is on becoming still through concentration on a word (or mantra), which is repeated faithfully, lovingly and continually.

Centering Prayer is another contemporary method of silent prayer that has become widely taught and used by millions around the world. Centering Prayer was developed by Thomas Keating, a Cistercian (Trappist) monk from St Benedict's monastery in Colorado. His book *Open Mind, Open Heart* has sold over half a million copies in English and has been translated into a number of foreign-language editions. Here the emphasis is on surrender and letting go, rather than concentration. I personally have found that the guidelines for Centering Prayer have helped me enormously in keeping a daily practice of silent prayer. The guidelines are very simple:

1 Choose a sacred word as the symbol of your intention to consent to God's presence and action within. The sacred word is chosen during a brief period of prayer to the Holy Spirit. We may use a word such as God, Jesus, *abba*, love, peace or trust. The sacred word is sacred not because of its inherent meaning, but because of the meaning we give it as the expression of our intention to consent.
2 Sitting comfortably and with eyes closed, settle briefly and then silently introduce the sacred word as the symbol of your consent to God's presence and action within.
3 When engaged with your thoughts, return ever-so-gently to the sacred word.
4 At the end of the prayer period, remain in silence with eyes closed for a couple of minutes.[44]

This method of prayer is about simply being with God. Normally we would aim for a period of 20 minutes to be still in the presence of God, with a 'naked intent toward God, the desire for him alone', as described in the 14th-century spiritual classic *The Cloud of Unknowing*.[45] This is our intention, the intention of our hearts before God. Of course, we will find ourselves aware of distractions and trains of thought that draw us away from this. Such 'thoughts are an inevitable, integral and normal part of Centering Prayer'.[46] Gently, as a feather on the breath of God, we return to the sacred word, to the still centre. There is no condemnation, no judgement, no such thing as a 'bad' time of Centering Prayer, or indeed a 'good' time of Centering Prayer. The important thing is just turning up, just doing it. It is about simply *being* in the presence of God.

A good way of learning to practise Centering Prayer is by using the Centering Prayer app, which is now widely available. The app allows you to choose, among other things, the duration of the silence and the beginning and ending sounds for the time of prayer.

The practice of contemplative prayer is not complicated. But that is not to say it is easy. It may sound straightforward to suggest that all we need to do is sit still in the presence of God for 20 minutes each day. But most, if not all, of us know that we can find all kinds of ways and reasons not to do this, and not to keep this time as a regular daily practice. Maybe we are too busy; maybe this kind of prayer seems to be a waste of our time. What is the point of just doing nothing for 20 minutes? That, in a way, is exactly the point. By doing nothing, we are giving our whole attention to God. We are offering God our whole being without any agenda of our own. We empty ourselves, following the model of Jesus (see Philippians 2:5–7). We let go of all self-interest and self-concern, and open our hearts to the one who loves us with a love that is as deep as the ocean, as vast as the open sky.

I am sure that some form of daily contemplative practice is essential if our hearts are to be deeply open to the Holy Spirit. If we are to be enabled to live in the freedom of Jesus, and to know our hearts radically transformed by his heart of love, we must spend time daily in a loving attentiveness to his holy presence. There is no other way.

Our lives may be full and busy, but that is all the more reason why it is important for us to have a daily discipline that helps us to maintain a measure of interior silence. We need this point of reference, this returning to the centre, in order to be attentive to God in all that we are doing. If our desire is that our lives should be pleasing to God in every way, we will be greatly strengthened by this practice. If we long to do God's will and to give ourselves fully to his service, we must find time in our daily routine for silence.

It is important to say that a contemplative response is not a withdrawal from the world or an opting out of the demands, busyness and stress of modern life. It is, in fact, the only way to remain true to Christ and to our own hearts as we engage in serving him in a complex and demanding world. Perhaps our greatest need is to be able, in the midst of all our work, to know an abiding sense of God's peace and presence and to be able to call upon him for help in any and every situation.

There is a short contemplative prayer, based on Psalm 40:13, that can be used for this purpose many times during the day and night: 'O God, make speed to save us; O Lord, make haste to help us.' The Christian monk and theologian John Cassian (c. 360–433) describes this prayer as the formula for contemplation that 'was given us by a few of the oldest Fathers who remained. To maintain an unceasing recollection of God it is to be ever set before you.' He goes on to say:

> This verse has been rightly selected from the whole Bible for this purpose. It fits every mood and temper of human nature, every temptation, every circumstance. It contains an invocation of God, a humble confession of faith, a reverent watchfulness, a meditation upon our frailty, confidence in God's answer, an assurance of his ever-present support.[47]

Our goal in all of this is to please God in everything we do. 'We keep before our minds the aim of pleasing him,' says St Basil (c. 329–379), another of the early church fathers. He says:

> Thus in the midst of our work we can fulfil the duty of prayer, giving thanks to him who has granted strength to our hands for performing our tasks, and cleverness to our minds for acquiring knowledge… thus we acquire a recollected spirit, when in every action we beg from God the success of our labours and satisfy our debt of gratitude to him… and when we keep before our minds the aim of pleasing him.[48]

Contemplative practice is not primarily about a particular method or system. It is rather an attitude of the heart, which is expressed in a way of life and in a daily discipline that holds us in attentiveness to the love of God. Each of us will need to find our own way, our own practice, that enables us to live faithfully before God, and to be true to ourselves and to our own desire to serve and honour him. We find our own practice, and we seek the grace of God to keep this practice, and to maintain this wherever possible.

Because this is a matter of the heart, where our deepest desires are involved, we will need to be accountable to others, to fellow pilgrims who are trustworthy and who care for us. We need wise companions, and those who are skilled in the art of discernment. The key in the development of this practice is the ability to recognise God's grace and his unfolding will and purpose for us. We need someone who can help us to be truthful with ourselves and with our motives and behaviour.

This is where finding a spiritual director or soul friend is so important. Then we will be able to come to a person who is 'on our side', who can help us to see what the Holy Spirit is up to in our lives. A good spiritual director will have experience from their own life and from the lives of those around them of seeing God at work, and of knowing that God is to be trusted completely in all his ways. Thus we can be guided, supported and given the encouragement and assurance that we need as we journey with God into a deeper integrity and obedience before him.

There are potentially many pitfalls and sources of discouragement and difficulty. Our false self will not easily allow us to 'let go' and empty ourselves before God. Contemplative practice is not about how I feel or what results I am seeing. It is not a win-lose, achievement-based activity. We are not seeking supernatural signs or mystical experiences. We are not seeking anything except the surrender of our hearts and lives to God. The real fruit of this will be the fruit of the Holy Spirit: love, joy, peace, patience, kindness, generosity, faithfulness, gentleness and self-control (Galatians 5:22–23). The measure of our practice will be our growth into the likeness and character of Jesus. Our practice must lead us to a greater love and service of others, if it is genuinely centred on Jesus and not on our own experience and self-interest. This is not about my reward or my spiritual experiences, but about yielding to the Holy Spirit. This is all that matters in contemplative prayer.

In contemplation, we throw ourselves upon God in radical faith and dependence on him. We trust God in the darkness, where we have let go of our own desires for control, status and security. There are likely to be times when we feel deeply uncomfortable, and we may cling to any reason not to enter this arena. We may say that we have theological problems about this form of prayer, or we may say that it just doesn't work for me. Many people in our society are uncomfortable with any form of extended silence. It takes courage to sit still in the midst of all the storms of life, to let go of trying to think about the solutions and the issues, to wait and do nothing and let God be God in our hearts.

The way through is faith. If God is God, and his ways are not our ways, we can surely, for a short period in each day, stop and place everything unconditionally in his hands. Contemplation is all about the life of faith, about depending completely on God for all our needs, for everything. We allow the Holy Spirit to pray in us, in prayer that is beyond words, in our own weakness and helplessness before God (see Romans 8:26–27).

Thomas Merton writes:

> The New Testament does not offer us techniques and expedients: it tells us to turn to God, to depend on his grace, to realise that the Spirit is given to us, wholly, in Christ. That he prays in us when we do not know how to pray: 'If the Spirit of him who raised Jesus from the dead dwells in you, he who raised Christ Jesus from the dead will give life to your mortal bodies also through his Spirit which dwells in you... For all who are led by the Spirit of God are sons of God. For you did not receive the spirit of slavery to fall back into fear, but you received the spirit of sonship. When we cry 'Abba! Father!' it is the Spirit himself bearing witness with our spirit that we are children of God.... Likewise the Spirit helps us in our weakness; for we do not know how to pray as we ought, but the Spirit himself intercedes for us with sighs too deep for words. And he who searches the heart knows what is the mind of the Spirit, because the Spirit intercedes for the saints according to the will of God (Romans 8:11, 14–16, 26–27).[49]

So, in contemplative practice we train ourselves to live from the heart not the head. We give our hearts to God in love. We allow the Holy Spirit to pray for us and in us, with sighs too deep for words. We cry, 'Abba, Father!' Through this prayer and this practice, we learn day by day to trust and depend on God for everything.

12

Truthfulness and self-knowledge

Early in 2015, I was interested to read that in the Episcopal Diocese of Western Massachusetts, the bishop and two senior clergy were offering a Lenten 'Un-quiet Day' on the theme of 'Bruce Springsteen: Prophet of Hope'. I had worked in the diocese on a summer programme when I was training for ministry, so I contacted Canon Rich Simpson and discussed the possibility of doing a similar event in the Diocese of Salisbury, where I was working as coordinator of spirituality. In February 2016, Peter Greenwood and I led our own 'Un-quiet Day', as a preparation for Lent in our diocese. We played some of Bruce Springsteen's music, and we talked about the way in which Springsteen's lyrics can help us live lives of truthfulness, courage and hope in the real world, out in the streets, and in the real life that goes on both out there and in our own hearts.

In his sermon at the Eucharist at the Un-Quiet Day in Western Massachusetts, Simpson said:

> Lent is an invitation to return to God with all our hearts. In a few moments we'll gather at the table where all are welcome – as we truly are: *spare parts and broken hearts*. So ultimately I think the purpose of an Un-Quiet Day is the same as that of a traditional Quiet Day: it is an invitation to the observance of a holy Lent 'by self-examination and repentance, by prayer, fasting and self-denial, and by reading and meditating on God's holy Word' (*Book of Common Prayer*). We might add that a little Springsteen can't hurt either.[50]

We can only come to God as we are, in spirit and in truth. The contemplative heart is a heart that has been moulded and trained, by joy and by suffering, to grow in self-knowledge and in truthfulness before God. In order for this to happen we need times of self-examination, repentance and prayer, and sometimes also fasting and self-denial. We also will need to go to the Bible, to incline our ears and hearts to God's holy word. Christians have always known that the primary way in which God speaks to us is through the Bible, as we allow the word of God to soak into us and to make the truth about God known to our hearts.

The gospel reading that was chosen for the Un-Quiet Day in Massachusetts was Matthew 6:1–6, the reading often used on Ash Wednesday, at the beginning of Lent. In this reading, Jesus warns of the danger of giving alms and praying in public in order that we may be praised by others. Simpson commented in his sermon:

> Today's gospel reading reminds us what happens when religious people take to the streets as posers rather than repairers of the breach, as people with hollow words but no actions to back those words up, as people who are holier than thou. The world does not need a church this Lent, or any time of the year, to be sent out into the world to be more pious, so that we can be seen giving alms in the streets and praying on the street corners. *The world needs us to be neighbours.* As Pope Francis put it this past November, the church must be reformed to create a more missionary and merciful church that gets its hands dirty as it seeks out the poor and oppressed.[51]

What is at stake here is the integrity of our faith, and of our claim to be authentic followers of Jesus Christ. If we are playing a role in order to appear to be religious or devout, our words and actions are hollow and will have little effect on bringing the love of Jesus to those in need. Self-examination and the desire for truthfulness before God are essential in the formation of a contemplative heart.

It is important to recognise that being Christian does not remove us from the struggles, pain and frailty of ordinary people. Being 'religious' has too often meant being 'holier than thou'. As Simpson says, 'The world needs us to be neighbours.' Many of Springsteen's songs are about the world of working people, especially men, who find that life is hard and full of disappointment, but who nonetheless find courage and joy in facing their own limitations and broken dreams and in looking for a way to build something that endures. Springsteen's lyrics are redolent of the bars, streets and factories of New Jersey, but they are also steeped in references to his Roman Catholic roots and upbringing. They draw us to the reality of the world in which we live, and they ask some searching questions about how we choose to deal with, and sometimes to avoid, the difficulties of life.

It seems to me that we can learn much from what Springsteen is saying to us in his music. I see Bruce Springsteen as a prophet of hope for our time. There are a number of reasons why it is worth paying attention to his lyrics.

Firstly, Springsteen helps us to face and to deal with whatever life brings. In his song 'When You're Alone', he says, 'There's things that'll knock you down you don't even see coming.'[52] Life is full of these kind of things, those unforeseen events, and often they are tough to handle. We make our plans; we think we are in control. But life throws stuff at us that we neither want nor expect, and it stops us doing all that we have planned for ourselves. We see this all the time in church ministry. We do not know what tomorrow will bring. Out of the blue, in the lives of the people in our churches, there are illnesses, bereavements, marriage problems, financial problems, and so on. None of us is immune. When something like this happens to us, and life takes an unexpected and probably unwelcome turn, what do we do? Springsteen's songs speak of this again and again. Sometimes this leads to despair and darkness, but often it leads to hope and change.

Secondly, Springsteen tells us that the temptation that many of us face when life gets difficult is avoidance or denial. In 'Hungry Heart', Springsteen sings:

> Got a wife and kids in Baltimore, Jack
> I went out for a ride and I never went back
> Like a river that don't know where it's flowing
> I took a wrong turn and I just kept going[53]

Most of us will know people who have taken a wrong turn and just kept going. Some of us will have done it ourselves. I think of my friend Philip. He was a good man, I thought – hard-working, faithful, a solid family man. But no one could ever tell Philip that he was wrong or that he had made a mistake. Phil was always right. One day Philip was offered a job in another town, in a different part of the country. His wife didn't want to move so far away, but Phil was convinced that this was his big opportunity and that he would soon make a lot of money in the new job. The plan was that he could come home every second weekend, and sometimes he would be able to work from home for a week. But after a few months, Phil stopped coming home. He was too busy, and the job was more complicated than he had realised. A few months passed, then a year, then another year. When Phil did occasionally come home, things were very difficult. After five years his marriage was over, and Phil found himself living with someone else, estranged from his wife and kids, and without a job. He took a wrong turn and he just kept going.

Denial is so dangerous, and it often leads to tragedy. Underlying our stubborn denial, for many of us, is a deep-seated fear of being known for who we really are. Denial may also be a kind of pride that keeps us from facing the truth about ourselves and our behaviour. Even the concern and advice of those who care about us and love us dearly can become unwelcome and threatening. When we are thinking about temptation, we also need to think about denial and avoidance.

Thirdly, Springsteen looks again and again in his songs at what people do with the reality of what life gives them. In his song 'Human Touch', he says, 'In the end what you don't surrender, well, the world just strips away.'[54] We have to learn to bend, to let go, to surrender. It's what Christians call humility. To be humble is to be known for who I really am. Again, this is about truthfulness: truthfulness with those around us, but above all, truthfulness with ourselves. We have to meet God as we are. There is no other way. A certain truthfulness is required of us if we are going to get through in life. If I can find that truthfulness, sometimes with the help of friends and counsellors, this will bring a light to shine into the dark corners of my own soul, and enable me to resist denial and the ways of the false self that thrive on denial. Then I can try to face some unpalatable truths about myself and my behaviour, and I can open myself to the grace of God and the fruit of the Holy Spirit. We learn, slowly but surely, to bend, to give in, to yield, and to let go and let God be God. It seems to me that this is the key to so much of what life brings, especially the unwelcome and the unforeseen.

Fourthly, Springsteen shows us how this struggle towards truthfulness leads us to an ever-deepening self-knowledge. In order to grow in maturity in Christ, we have to find our true selves and give up striving to be something or someone that God never made us to be in the first place. Springsteen's song 'Brilliant Disguise' is very telling. In the 1980s, Bruce Springsteen fell in love with Julianne Phillips, an actor and model, and they were married in 1985. But the relationship didn't work out, and they were divorced a few years later. In 'Brilliant Disguise', Springsteen writes about himself during this difficult time:

> Struggling to do everything right, and then it all falls apart when out go the lights
> So when you look at me, you better look hard and look twice
> Is that me baby or just a brilliant disguise?[55]

There is a depth of truthfulness here that recognises that none of us can know all the time what our motives are and why we do some of the things we do. None of us really knows ourselves that well, and often other people can see sides of us that we simply cannot see for ourselves. We are living with masks and disguises. How can we trust one another when some of the time we don't even trust ourselves?

But the Holy Spirit leads us to live more and more from our own true selves, in truthfulness before God and one another, especially those closest to us. Contemplative prayer is the place I have found where much of this work is rooted, and that is why I come back to this again and again. When I let go of my own agenda and open myself unconditionally to God in silence, a deep work of transformation begins to take place. It can be painful and costly, and we may try to avoid the struggle of presenting ourselves in this way to God. But as we make this our daily practice, our hearts are changed within us, and a true humility, an honesty and a compassion for ourselves and others is nurtured within us.

Springsteen speaks to us from the streets and the factories, from 'the spare parts and broken hearts that keep the world turnin' around'.[56] He helps us not to withdraw into pious religion. I once heard Terry Wogan, the broadcaster and television personality, speaking in an interview about his Catholic upbringing in Limerick, Ireland. He said that there was a lot of religion all around him, but not much faith. The way of Jesus is not to hide in the safety of our beautiful buildings, with our lovely music and ritual and religious language and safe conversations. Bruce Springsteen is a prophet of hope who calls us out into the streets, where real life is to be found. We can be people of hope because we know that as we face what is really going on in our own hearts, and what life is like for people in the real world, this is where Jesus is to be found.

13

Learning to live in the present moment

A few years ago, when I was working as coordinator of spirituality in Salisbury Diocese, I helped to lead a series of day events for those in ministry and leadership on various aspects of becoming a contemplative minister. Together with Sue Langdon and Peter Greenwood, I looked at how we might learn to lead churches in a contemplative pattern, beginning with our own daily practice of prayer and stillness. Increasingly I became aware that a contemplative model of ministry raises many wider issues for those in leadership. We are confronted with the need to examine our own behaviour and habits, and to recognise the pull of the false self and our desires for control, security and significance as we tackle the day-to-day challenges of life in ministry. These self-focused concerns and desires can shape our whole approach to leadership. We may find that much of our ministry is actually about 'me'.

Becoming a contemplative minister means learning to wake up to the true self in us, and allowing our true selves to direct our public activity and leadership. This, for many of us, requires a radical shift in our approach to leadership. The fruitfulness of our ministry is far more dependent on who we are than on what, or how much, we do. Being comes before doing. Finding my true self means finding who I am called by God to be, rather than what I am called by God to do.

As we learn to lead from the still centre, we will find that we are more able to be fully present to the person or group of people with whom we are speaking or meeting. We live in the present, taking in all that this moment holds and offers to us. We are not living in the past, dwelling on what has happened to us, or in the future, calculating our response to whatever may be coming next. We meet each moment as it comes to us, and accomplish in that moment all that belongs to it.

The restless heart always wants to be somewhere else apart from where I am. Learning to live in the present moment shows us that we do not need to calculate and quantify in order to appreciate what we have. There is no need to compare; we can just enjoy the moment, without always wondering what comes next.

During one of the 'Contemplative Minister' days, Sue Langdon spoke about Centering Prayer and the problem of distracting trains of thought that take over when we are trying to be still. She said that in the moment we realise our thoughts have drifted off, what happens is that the *true self* wakes up to the false self, which has taken us off on some train of thought. Then we use a sacred word or phrase that we have previously chosen to return gently to the still centre, to the *true self*.

I thought at the time that this was very significant. In Centering Prayer, what we are doing is learning to live from the true self, which I now realise also means learning to live in the present moment. This is a central issue for me, because this brings me back to my own moment-by-moment trust and confidence in God's love and care. I am now discovering that when we return to rest in the true self, we are trusting completely in the love of God; we are letting go and placing ourselves completely in his hands, and this is where we find our true freedom and peace.

The love of God for each of us in Christ Jesus is something that we may read about many times in the Bible, and may have understood and accepted in our minds. Yet for this extraordinary truth of God's unfailing love in Christ to change and rule our hearts, we have to go deeper than intellectual assent and understanding. For the apostle Paul this was the reality that ruled every aspect of his life and witness. He knew within his own heart that nothing would ever be able to separate him from the love of God in Christ Jesus. He wrote:

> Who will separate us from the love of Christ? Will hardship, or distress, or persecution, or famine, or nakedness, or peril, or sword?... No, in all these things we are more than conquerors through him who loved us.
>
> ROMANS 8:35, 37

When we are under pressure, ill, in trouble or under attack or persecution, when we are most in need, we may find ourselves thrashing about, struggling to survive and crying out to God to help us. This, says Paul, is when we depend directly on the love of Christ. He will not fail us or forsake us:

> For I am convinced that neither death, nor life, nor angels, nor rulers, nor things present, nor things to come, nor powers, nor height, nor depth, nor anything else in all creation, will be able to separate us from the love of God in Christ Jesus our Lord.
>
> ROMANS 8:38–39

This is the ultimate reality.

In becoming my true self, I can simply be the person I am, just as I am, totally depending on God, who knows me and loves me as I am. This is the place where I know that I am loved and accepted by God, regardless of the circumstances or difficulties I find myself in, and where I do not have to prove *anything* or achieve *anything*. I let go and let God be God.

This has huge implications. I have been discovering how this rootedness in God's love in Christ works out in real life. As I have become more committed to this way of living, I have become aware of a number of ways in which my false self likes to run the show. When I am driving, for example, I sometimes find myself racing the other drivers who go past, and I have to say to myself, 'Ian, this isn't a race.' But I know that sometimes it is my false self that is in the driving seat, and off I go. I soon slow down again, and I try to recognise what is happening and just smile and say to myself, 'Oh, Ian!' I know that this is how I am, and that's okay. Learning to live in the present moment means being compassionate with myself and not having to prove anything to anyone else.

We can learn a lot from our reactions when we are out on the road. When I see a green light about to change to orange and red, I tend to want to speed up and rush through, and keep up with all the other cars. My wife, on the other hand, is a more cautious driver. When she thinks that a green light is about to change, she slows down. Sometimes, if I am a passenger, I find myself saying, either silently or aloud, 'Go, go, go!' What is this all about? It is surely about my wanting often to rush on to the next thing instead of stopping in the present moment. How often, I wonder, when someone has been telling me about some pain or difficulty in their lives, have I tried to quickly move on to a solution, instead of waiting and listening to the other person?

There are numerous other habits and behaviour patterns that I have developed that keep me occupied with my desires for control, security and significance. There's the compulsive activity – looking at the iPad and the iPod or watching the television and the news media, the constant distraction with something to occupy a restless mind. I have countless strategies that keep me from the restfulness of simple contentment with who I am and with God's love and goodness towards me. There is also my preoccupation with calculating and with numbers. I count the money I have spent and the money I have earned. I count the number of bird and animal species I have seen this year. I count the days and weeks, which is probably related to my eleven years at boarding school, where we counted the days and weeks to the next school holiday or long weekend. I measure and I calculate. This seems to be the default position of dealing with modern life. We count time and money, as though this somehow gives us control of our lives. We measure goods, targets and achievements in every aspect of life. This is how many contemporary workplaces and management practices operate.

Then there is my habit of talking over and over about the same pet subjects, and holding on to mostly small and insignificant grievances. It may be about the medical care system, the church or the days of leave that I have forfeited. I am also aware of my avoidance of depth. Somehow, I find ways of not making time for things that I know to be important – prayer; reading the books that I have bought; and visiting friends, neighbours or members of our church who are in need.

Where does all this come from? I have come to see that a lot of this is tied up with the false self and its habits. The false self needs to be in control. If I am in control, I feel safe and secure, even for just a very short while. The false self also needs to feel important, to know that I matter, that my life is significant and that it counts for something. Measuring my achievements and my goals is a means of telling this part of me that I am succeeding, that I am still okay and somehow keeping my life on track. My first reaction in any complex or challenging situation is usually about 'me', about my interests, my security, my significance. When these are threatened in any way, the defensive response of the false self kicks in. I want and need to be in control. But a life of faith requires that I recognise I am not in control and I depend upon God for everything. As long as my reactions are all about my need for control, about calculating, defending and protecting my interests, I cannot respond with the compassion, patience and trust that are the fruit of the Holy Spirit. I cannot be fully present to God or to the other person or people before me.

I am learning that while the 'me-first' self is still very much alive, there is a deeper reality of who I am: my true self, the person that I am in Christ, held secure in the unfailing, unconditional love of God. I can look with compassion on my false self, because I now know that this false self is not my master. My life is ruled by grace and by mercy, the mercy of God in Christ. I aim to return as often as I can, at different points during the day, to rest in the mercy and compassion of my Lord. 'For thus said the Lord God, the Holy One of Israel: In returning and rest you shall be saved; in quietness and in trust shall be your strength' (Isaiah 30:15).

As we learn to be present to God, to ourselves and to the other, here and now, we find that a new fruitfulness becomes apparent in our hearts and our lives. We grow in our attentiveness to God, to the whispers of the Holy Spirit. We notice things that we may well have missed previously, because we were too busy or too distracted. We learn to listen in new ways.

We find ourselves seeing the people around us with new eyes. As I was sitting quietly in a busy supermarket coffee shop a few weeks ago, I looked around me, and I knew: God loves everyone here, just as much as he loves me. He loves us all, all these people with their supermarket trolleys and crying babies and walking aids, with an infinite love, way beyond any human understanding. This was not an epiphany or blinding revelation, just a deep awareness, which changes the way I see people, especially strangers. This is the fruit of learning to live from this still centre, not from the 'me-first' centre. We look out and we see people around us and we smile, and we say to ourselves, 'What a wonderful world.'

At other times we look out at our world and those around us, and we grieve. Our hearts are touched in new ways by the pain of others. This love is a love that knows both joy and sorrow. It is the love that we see in the anguish of a mother for her infant child crying out in pain, perhaps from the needle of their first injection or from teething, tears filling her eyes as she sees her baby suffer. This is the love that is so moved by the awfulness of rough-sleeping in the middle of an icy winter that it knows something must be done, and that it starts with me. I have to do something, whatever I can do.

We find in the present moment a new sense of gratitude, of thankfulness for all that is, all that has been and all that will be. We take time to enjoy the beauty of the day. We find interior silence, the peace that passes understanding. We find rest, rest for our souls, as we abide in Christ, letting go of all that pulls us away from his love for us. 'As the Father has loved me, so I have loved you; abide in my love' (John 15:9).

The false self clings to control, security and significance. These are but illusions, mere shadows of the true and the eternal, which are ours in Christ. In Christ we find our true security and safety, true significance, true peace and contentment. We are given the peace that the world cannot give. When this peace rules our hearts, we find that our hearts are set to obey his holy, good and just commandments. We find also that we are defended by him from anxiety and the fear of our enemies.

Though we live in troubled times, and confusion and suffering are all around us, we are able to pass our time in rest and quietness. Our hearts are held in the love of Christ, and so we know 'all is well, and all shall be well, and all manner of things shall be well'.[57]

The collect for peace[58]

> O God, from whom all holy desires, all good counsels, and all just
>   works do proceed:
> Give unto thy servants that peace which the world cannot give;
> that both our hearts may be set to obey thy commandments,
> and also that by thee we being defended from the fear of our
>   enemies
> may pass our time in rest and quietness;
> through the merits of Jesus Christ our Saviour.
> Amen

14

Contemplation and action

We are a contemplative Augustinian Community and our principal work is worship, thanksgiving and intercession, reaching out on behalf of others to the source of all love and goodness and holding before Christ the pain and suffering of the world.

Burnham Abbey: The Society of the Precious Blood[59]

Contemplation leads to transformation. As we grow in our contemplative practice, we are changed, and we find ourselves being moved by the Holy Spirit to see the world in the light of God's love for all that he has made. Our hearts are softened, and we weep with those who are weeping, even as we share in the joy of those who are blessed. Contemplation that is rooted in Jesus leads to action in his service.

The Bible speaks many times of the necessity of a change of mind or perception (*metanoia*) and a change and purifying of the heart (Psalm 51:10; Ezekiel 36:26; Matthew 5:8; 22:37). We are to 'not be conformed to this world, but be transformed by the renewing of your minds, so that you may discern what is the will of God – what is good and acceptable and perfect' (Romans 12:2).

I have often seen and experienced the close links between contemplation, action and transformation in my work with the church in southern Africa. Many South African Christian leaders I have known have been men and women of deep and disciplined prayer, whose Christian commitment has led them directly to the needs of the poor. I can think of many examples: Desmond Tutu, Peter Kerchoff, Beyers Naudé and many others. Some are well known, but many are those who have quietly and courageously given their lives to God and to the service of the poor, the desperate, the oppressed and the broken around them, without ever being widely known or recognised.

Sister Diana SPB (Society of the Precious Blood) spent 45 years in Lesotho as an Anglican sister, first in the capital, Maseru, and then in Masite. Sister Diana had come to Lesotho from England with a strong sense that God had called her to southern Africa and to its people. I became aware of Sister Diana and her work because for 15 years I was a trustee of the Southern African Church Development Trust (SACDT), which raised money in the UK to support the work of the church in southern Africa. Our aim was to make a difference to ordinary people, by giving opportunity, health education and spiritual support through the local churches. We were involved in a number of projects in Lesotho, and we relied upon Sister Diana as someone who knew first-hand the needs of the local people and whom we could trust to see that all funds directly reached those for whom they were intended.

In 2007 I visited Lesotho with a group from the church where I was rector, St Peter's Yaxley. We had given, through SACDT and Sister Diana, a large sum of money to help build a new church in Maseru. So in June of that year I was able to visit her at the Masite mission, and to see for myself this contemplative community perched on a remote and dusty corner of one of the poorest countries on earth.

Lesotho is a beautiful mountain kingdom in the centre of southern Africa, completely landlocked by its much larger and richer neighbour, South Africa. Lesotho is also a place of poverty and immense human need. At 620 deaths in every 100,000 live births, Lesotho has one of the highest maternal mortality rates in the world.[60] A major problem is the long distance people have to travel for medical care. Many people might have to walk for eight hours to reach a health centre, which they are dependent on not only for medical treatment but also to gain access to other services, such as condoms. If people have to walk eight hours to get a condom, there is a strong possibility of engaging in unprotected sex, which makes HIV prevention very difficult, especially where the infection rate is so high. In Lesotho 23% of the general population is HIV-positive and for pregnant mothers the prevalence is 27%.[61] Poverty and disease become a vicious circle, with serious consequences for children, young people and families.

Sister Diana is now 85 years old. The community house in Masite closed in 2014 and she now lives in a small village in West Sussex. I recently visited her there and spoke to her about her life and her call to be a contemplative and to spend most of her life in such a remote corner of Africa. I asked her how she came to join the Society of the Precious Blood, an Anglican contemplative community with convents in England, Lesotho and South Africa.

Sister Diana said to me:

> From the beginning I have always had a yen for the contemplative life, and I also had a yen for South Africa. My call was to give my life completely back to God. When I was young I heard the story of Hannah in the Bible, giving her son Samuel back to God. I became vividly aware that God had gifted me with a life and I could choose to spend it as he wanted or as I wanted. I then gave my life back to God, and from then on I was searching as to what would be next. I was confirmed when I was 14, and I always had a drawing to prayer. I was very involved in the church and was trained as a Sunday school teacher. All this time I was searching, and one day the diocesan lady who was leading the training said to me, 'Diana, why don't you come to our retreat?' I went, and I learnt for the first time about the religious life in the Church of England. Soon I was saying that I wanted to be a sister.

> My mother was telling everyone that I was going to be a missionary teacher. But I realised that if God wanted everything,

I had to give up the missionary part and the Africa part, and everything. It had to be God alone. I then came across a copy of St Teresa of Avila's *Way of Perfection*, and that really spoke to me. So I plodded on, and I decided to go to the Community of the Holy Name, because they were the nearest to me. They sent me first to Liberia, and then to St Catherine's in Maseru in Lesotho.

When I found the Society of the Precious Blood at Masite, it all came together. There I was in Africa, and there was the contemplative life that I have always desired. I then had to come back to England for three months to get permission for the move to SPB. Then I went back to Africa and I felt that God was calling me to stay in Africa until I died, as I thought!

I asked Sister Diana what it was about the distinctively contemplative life at SPB and Masite that made her want to go there. She said to me, 'I wanted to go deeper into prayer and to have more time for prayer. But it didn't work out like that, because my gifts were needed for all the other things.'

Sister Diana was sure that God was calling her to make prayer the centre of her life, of everything, which is why she joined a contemplative community. But she soon discovered that life in Masite was not simply about prayer. Although as contemplative sisters, the members of the community did not go out from Masite to work among the local people, they found that many people came to them with needs and requests for help. 'Until free primary healthcare and free primary education came in, many families would come to us for help,' Sister Diana told me. 'I was receiving money from the sisters in Oxford for school shoes, for very basic needs in many of the families.'

I explained to Sister Diana that when I visited the community at Masite, what I found so striking was that although there was clearly a strong commitment to the life of prayer, this was also the community to whom we at SACDT could send money that was being raised in the UK, knowing that it would go to the most needy, the most vulnerable, the very poorest. Sister Diana explained that in this she worked closely with Mr Lebuso, the headmaster of St Barnabas secondary school in Masite, which was close to the convent.

> Mr Lebuso and I worked together on who should be helped, and who shouldn't. We didn't go out; people came to us with their needs. And in the beginning we had to give out quite a lot of money. But then we had an excellent nurse clinician who came to the clinic which had started in our garden as a mother-and-baby clinic. This was started by one of our original South African sisters. At the beginning there was no clinic, and the guest mistress used to give out medicines, and the payment was simply to carry some stones to build a wall. People knew that if they came to the community they would receive fair help.

From these small beginnings the clinic slowly developed and expanded to meet the needs that were growing steadily in the local area. Now, although the SPB community is no longer there, there is in Masite an excellent medical centre, the St Barnabas Anglican Health Centre, which is well equipped and provides primary healthcare for thousands of local Basotho people. Sister Diana said:

> Our little mother-and-baby clinic, with Sister Helen and food from CAFOD and medicines from Scott Hospital in Morija, has turned into a full-sized health centre with lying-in facilities, a nurse clinician in charge, three other registered nurses, three practical nurses, counsellors, a driver and a vehicle given by a fund from the Community of the Resurrection.

Sister Diana's work and responsibilities were also changing and growing:

> I transferred to SPB in 1976, when Bishop Desmond Tutu was our bishop in Lesotho. For the first few years I was still learning

in the community. But in 1980 we set up a house of prayer in Kimberley in South Africa, about 250 miles away. At that time I was made bursar, and I was also the main driver between the two houses. I was doing a tremendous amount of work: I was the sacristan, and I was even put in charge of the kitchen, but I couldn't cope with that as well.

I asked her, 'How did you balance all of that with your call to prayer?' She replied:

I found it very difficult and at times disappointing. But I think I accepted it as part of God's will for me, because it had to be done. I did have my retreats and so on. That side of my life was guarded. Also, there was music. I was a lead singer, so I was singing the office and the daily mass, and this gave me a framework of support. Music has always been a great enabler for prayer for me. Music takes me to a place of stillness, and sometimes it really uplifted me.

'So were you able to reconcile the contemplation and the action?' I asked her.

'Yes,' she said. 'Because grace builds on human nature. But as a contemplative you work jolly hard.'

I asked Sister Diana to tell me about the contemplative life of the community. She explained:

We started with Lauds at 6.00 am, if not earlier, and an early mass. Then we had breakfast followed by Terce, and also an hour of silent prayer. But often that hour was just gone because of all the things that had to be done. And, of course, there were the other daily offices. It was very frustrating when I had to miss the offices and the silent prayer, but I learnt to accept it. My main aim was always to become the person that God wanted me to be.

As I listened to Sister Diana, I could see that being a contemplative meant asking, again and again, 'What does God want me to become? What is God asking of me in this situation?' It is Sister Diana's obedience to God that marks her out to me as someone who knows first-hand what a contemplative response means in the often difficult and challenging realities of our world. Being a contemplative is not an escape from reality: if anything, it is the opposite. 'The closer you get to God, the more you have God's compassionate heart,' says Sister Diana.

I asked Sister Diana what she has learnt from her life at Masite, where she lived for 41 years. She replied:

> I learnt a lot of compassion, and a lot of courage. I had to stand up in a number of instances when others didn't understand. For example, two of the older sisters said that certain children should not be helped because of the immorality of their mentally ill mother. They were helped, and they are still in touch with me. The second girl in the family is probably the most courageous person I have ever met. She is not just doing an important job in education but is also so courageous in her personal life, and has suffered so much.

> Being a contemplative helps one to know that God's love reaches even the most unfortunate, the most unlikely, the most despised. Our main call in SPB is intercessory prayer, and we kept a half-hour watch, each one in turn, throughout the day, every day, praying and interceding for the needs around us.

'God has been everything to me,' she said. 'I have been in high danger.'

'Southern Africa can be a dangerous place,' I said, remembering some of my own experiences of life in apartheid South Africa. Sister Diana knows this all too well:

Bishop Desmond Tutu and Bishop Simeon Nkoane used to come through to Lesotho to teach at the seminary. So we got to know them. Simeon Nkoane said to me, 'You are not to turn into a country bumpkin here!' He wanted me to go to Johannesburg for a while. I remember being at a retreat there, and I have never known anyone listen as Bishop Simeon did. He gave me a whole Saturday morning and he said, 'Just talk.' Then he drove me to a wedding in Soweto on the Saturday afternoon. I knew nothing about the permits that were required in those days. Simeon said, 'You must experience an African wedding.' As we were driving back to Johannesburg, luckily I was wearing black, because Simeon said, 'You mustn't turn your face. The Special Branch are on our tail, but I think I can shake them off.' And he did.

During those days, the Special Branch were everywhere, and because of the presence of the African National Congress (ANC) in Lesotho, and in Masite, there was always an awareness of being watched and knowing that danger and trouble could be just around the corner.

Masite is a beautiful place, but it is also a place of poverty, of isolation, of immense human need and sometimes of real danger and conflict. How does Sister Diana remember Masite, now that she has left and come back to England? She said:

It was primitive. For a long time we only had candlelight. It was beautiful too. I could go out and sit on the hillside, looking across to the mountains, and pray. I shall never forget the African skies, and how the weather can change, and the most colossal thunderstorms, and the beautiful October starlit nights.

I said to Sister Diana:

You had this call to a life of prayer and that led you to a life of serving those who are largely forgotten by the modern world, people who are often very poor and in very great need. And you have had to give of yourself at great cost and sometimes in great danger, as a contemplative, because that is what God's love has demanded of you. Is that a fair summary?

'Yes,' she replied. 'Yes.'

Conclusion

Interior silence

To contemplate is to gaze, to wonder, to behold. The word 'contemplate' has its origins in the Latin verb *contemplari*, based on *templum*, a place of observation or a building in which a deity resides. So to contemplate is to gaze upon God, and to wonder and behold, and therefore to rest, in the mystery of the one whose very nature is eternal love.

This is the starting point for the contemplative response to our distracted and driven world. We cease from rush, from compulsive activity, and we become still. We sit, we wonder and we soak in the one who is our peace, the peace that passes understanding. It is like soaking in a hot bath after a long and demanding day, and gradually allowing the strain and stress to ease away.

I recently went for a few days' silent retreat in a Benedictine abbey in Kent. As I settled myself into the retreat, leaving behind the busy motorways and the demands of the diary, I had a sense of leaving the world behind for a short while. Here, I felt, there is nothing to achieve, except to be quiet and to be alone. Here, there is nothing to acquire, no Wi-Fi or internet or shops. Here, there is no opportunity to indulge; there is only simple, nourishing food and drink. This is a place where Jesus says to the storm around me, 'Peace. Be still.'

I find that it takes me a day or so to adjust to the different rhythm of life in a place of retreat and silence. This can be challenging and difficult. There is a certain lack of 'normal' comfort, but I know that I need to let go and accept a measure of discomfort from time to time. This is necessary for the care of my soul, that I may come back to a renewed sense of the presence of God in my life. Here, at the abbey at West Malling, I have come to a place of sustained silence and prayer, from which I will not choose to quickly and easily escape. Here, God has hold of me, and I want to be available to him. My longing, my prayer, is that I may be renewed in my desire to nurture and guard this interior silence in all of my normal daily life.

Interior silence is the key to so much in the spiritual life. This is made clear in *The Rule of Taizé*, which sets out the foundations of the life of the Taizé community in France. *The Rule of Taizé* says:

> Maintain interior silence in all things in order to dwell in Christ. Interior silence requires first of all to forget one's self, to quiet discordant voices, and to master obsessing worry. Interior silence renders possible our conversation with Jesus Christ.

> But who does not fear this silence, and prefer diversion at the hour of work; and would not rather flee from prayer by tiring himself in vain tasks, forgetful of his neighbour and of himself?[62]

To abide or dwell in Christ, it is necessary to nurture our interior silence. This means that we must face the reality of the threat that is posed by our culture of speed and distraction and overload. A distracted culture buffets us and pulls us away from our central goal in life, which is to abide in Christ and to live Christlike lives.

Distraction and depth do not go well together. If we long to know more of the deep things of the Spirit of God, we will need to seek solitude and silence as a regular practice in our lives. A silent retreat offers the possibility of the purifying of our hearts and our desires. This usually involves some measure of cost and sacrifice, and maybe of suffering. My experience is that contemplation means boredom for the false self, and I have to actively resist the temptations to move away from depth, and busy myself with something trivial.

Here, at West Malling, I rise early and make my way across the grass and over the little stream to the chapel. It is a cold winter morning, but I know that God is here, in the stillness and in the quiet companionship of my fellow retreatants. In this place of prayer, I see the essence of who I am, my true self in Christ. I see also my desire for God, my human weakness and frailty, my dependence on God's grace and goodness, my gifts, my joys and my sorrows.

These are the truths on which is founded my life as God knows me and sees me. My life is not about acquiring, achieving and indulging. It does not matter how much I have done, or bought, or eaten. My life is hid with God in Christ. This is where I long to abide and rest.

Notes

1 Ian Cowley, *The Contemplative Minister* (BRF, 2015), p. 106.
2 Malcolm Muggeridge, *A Twentieth-Century Testimony*, quoted in Nicky Gumbel, *30 Days* (Alpha, 1999), p. 105.
3 Thomas Merton, *New Seeds of Contemplation* (New Directions, 1972), p. 34.
4 Robert Colvile, 'Fast fingers, quick steps, motor mouths', *The Sunday Times*, 27 March 2016.
5 Colvile, 'Fast fingers, quick steps, motor mouths'.
6 Trades Union Congress, '15 per cent increase in people working more than 48 hours a week risks a return to "Burnout Britain"', warns TUC', 9 September 2015, **tuc.org.uk/news/15-cent-increase-people-working-more-48-hours-week-risks-return-%E2%80%98burnout-britain%E2%80%99-warns-tuc**.
7 Nicholas Carr, *The Shallows: How the internet is changing the way we think, read and remember* (Atlantic Books, 2011); and 'Is the internet making you stupid?', *The Times*, 14 August 2010.
8 Nicholas Carr, 'Now what was I talking about?', *The Times*, 14 August 2010.
9 UCM conference report, 'Encounter 70', 10–16 July 1970, Wilgespruit.
10 Thomas Merton, *The Seven Storey Mountain* (Harcourt Brace and Company, 1948), p. 75.
11 Thomas Merton, *New Seeds of Contemplation* (New Directions Publishing, 1972), p. 1.
12 Merton, *New Seeds of Contemplation*, p. 21.
13 Merton, *New Seeds of Contemplation*, p. 31.
14 Church of the Province of Southern Africa, *An Anglican Prayer Book 1989* (Collins, 1989), p. 91.
15 Quoted in James Martin, *Becoming Who You Are* (Hidden Spring, 2005).
16 **payscale.com**, October 2017.
17 'Nurses get salary increment of between 10.4% and 28.5% for the year 2016', *Lusaka Times*, 15 October 2015, **lusakatimes.com/2015/10/15/nurses-get-salary-increment-of-between-10-4-and-28-5-for-the-year-2016**.

18 **payscale.com**, October 2017.

19 J.K. Galbraith, *The Affluent Society* (1958), quoted in *The Times*, 17 October 2017.

20 Dennis Okholm, *The Dictionary of Christian Spirituality* (Zondervan, 2011), p. 484.

21 Justin Welby, *Dethroning Mammon: Making money serve grace* (Bloomsbury, 2016), excerpted in 'A season to learn true value', *Church Times*, 3 March 2017, **churchtimes.co.uk/articles/2017/3-march/features/features/a-season-to-learn-true-value**.

22 Alan Storkey, 'Postmodernism is consumption', in Craig Bartholomew and Thorsten Mortiz (eds), *Christ and Consumerism: A critical analysis of the spirit of the age* (Pasternoster, 2000), pp. 100–01.

23 Jonathan Dean, 'Gimme Moore', *The Sunday Times* style magazine, 20 November 2016.

24 **dailymaverick.co.za**, 23 August 2017.

25 Andrea Tornielli, 'O come all ye faithful', *The Sunday Times*, 16 April 2017.

26 Alain de Botton, *Status Anxiety* (Hamish Hamilton, 2004), pp. 3–4.

27 Malcolm Muggeridge, *Tread Softly For You Tread on My Jokes* (Collins, 1966).

28 Ray Williams, 'Is it time to be more right-brained?', *Psychology Today*, 21 July 2010.

29 Brett Frischmann and Evan Selinger, 'Robots have already taken over our work, but they're made of flesh and bone', *The Guardian*, 25 September 2017, p. 25.

30 Howard Gray, *The New SCM Dictionary of Christian Spirituality* (SCM, 2005).

31 David Watson, *Fear No Evil* (Hodder and Stoughton, 1984), p. 171 (emphasis in original).

32 William H. Shannon, *Thomas Merton's Paradise Journey* (Burns and Oates, 2000), p. 72 (emphasis in original).

33 Shannon, *Thomas Merton's Paradise Journey*, p. 72.

34 Shannon, *Thomas Merton's Paradise Journey*, p. 73.

35 Shannon, *Thomas Merton's Paradise Journey*, p. 59.

36 J. Keith Miller, *Hope in the Fast Lane* (Harper, 1987), pp. 4–5.

37 Miller, *Hope in the Fast Lane*, pp. 5–6.

38 Miller, *Hope in the Fast Lane*, p. 6.

39 Miller, *Hope in the Fast Lane*, p. 86.

40 Miller, *Hope in the Fast Lane*, p. 258.

41 The Archbishop of Canterbury's address to the Thirteenth Ordinary General Assembly of the Synod of Bishops on The New Evangelism for the Transmission of the Christian Faith, October 2012.

42 Theophan the Recluse, quoted in Jean Khoury, 'Bringing the mind into the heart', Spirituality blog, 7 June 2014, **amorvincit.blogspot. com/2014/06/spirituality-108-bringing-mind-into.html**.

43 The World Community for Christian Meditation, 'Christian meditation in the UK', **christianmeditation.org.uk**.

44 Thomas Keating, *Open Mind, Open Heart*, 20th anniversary edition (Continuum, 2006), pp. 177–78. See also, Keating, 'The method of Centering Prayer', **contemplativeoutreach.org/sites/default/files/ private/center_prayer_method_2017-01_0.pdf**.

45 William Johnston (ed.), *The Cloud of Unknowing* (HarperCollins Fount, 1997), p. 22.

46 Keating, 'The method of Centering Prayer'.

47 John Cassian, *The Fire and the Cloud*, edited by David A. Fleming (Geoffrey Chapman, 1978), pp. 34–35.

48 Quoted in Thomas Merton, *Contemplative Prayer* (DLT, 2005), p. 35.

49 Merton, *Contemplative Prayer*, p. 48.

50 Canon Rich Simpson, 'Meet me out in the street: Bruce Springsteen Lenten Un-Quiet Day', transcript, 2015, quoting 'Spare Parts' by Bruce Springsteen and *The Book of Common Prayer* (emphasis in original).

51 Simpson, 'Meet me out in the street' (emphasis in original).

52 Bruce Springsteen, 'When You're Alone', 1987.

53 Bruce Springsteen, 'Hungry Heart', 1980.

54 Bruce Springsteen, 'Human Touch', 1992.

55 Bruce Springsteen, 'Brilliant Disguise', 1987.

56 Bruce Springsteen, 'Spare Parts', 1987.

57 Julian of Norwich, quoted in Dan Graves, 'Article 31: All shall be well', Christian History Institute, **christianhistoryinstitute.org/incontext/ article/julian**.

58 **churchofengland.org/prayer-and-worship/worship-texts-and-resources/book-common-prayer/order-evening-prayer**

59 **burnhamabbey.org**

60 'Médecins Sans Frontières calls it a day', *Lesotho Times*, 22 October 2015, **lestimes.com/medecins-sans-frontieres-calls-it-a-day**.

61 'Médecins Sans Frontières calls it a day'.

62 Communauté de Taizé, *The Rule of Taizé* (Les Presses de Taizé, 1968), pp. 53–54.

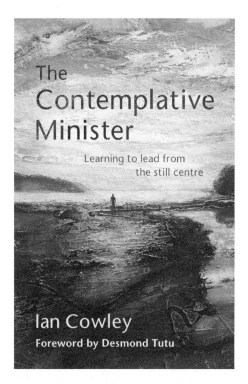

At one time Christian ministry offered the opportunity to spend your life in the study of God's word, in reading and reflection, in prayer and sermon preparation, and in the faithful pastoral care of a community. These days there are very few jobs in full-time ministry which do not require a heroic combination of stamina, multi-tasking and change management. Drawing on his experience of developing and leading relevant training programmes, Ian Cowley assesses the stresses and pressures of the job and shows how to grow into a 'contemplative minister', prioritising a relationship of deepening love with God.

The Contemplative Minister
Learning to lead from the still centre
Ian Cowley
978 0 85746 360 9 £8.99

brfonline.org.uk

'A written masterclass' Paul Wilcox

You are more important than your MINISTRY

SUSTAINING LEADERSHIP

PAUL SWANN

Many books on leadership and ministry are written from the point of view of success and strength. In *Sustaining Leadership*, Paul Swann writes out of the raw experience of failure, getting to the heart of who we are as leaders rather than what we do. From this he offers both hope and practical resources for sustaining effective long-term ministry, looking at self-care, balance and healthy ministry, feasting on divine love, and more. As he says, this is the best gift we can offer those we serve.

Sustaining Leadership
You are more important than your ministry
Paul Swann
978 0 85746 651 8 £8.99

brfonline.org.uk

Transforming
lives and communities

Christian growth and understanding of the Bible

Resourcing individuals, groups and leaders in churches for their own spiritual journey and for their ministry

Church outreach in the local community

Offering two programmes that churches are embracing to great effect as they seek to engage with their local communities and transform lives

Teaching Christianity in primary schools

Working with children and teachers to explore Christianity creatively and confidently

Children's and family ministry

Working with churches and families to explore Christianity creatively and bring the Bible alive

parenting for faith

Visit **brf.org.uk** for more information on BRF's work

brf.org.uk

The Bible Reading Fellowship (BRF) is a Registered Charity (No. 233280)